THE ULTIMATE GUIDE TO SHOTGUNNING

Guns, gear, and hunting tactics for deer, big game,
upland birds, waterfowl, and small game

DAVID R. HENDERSON

The Lyons Press
Guilford, Connecticut
An imprint of The Globe Pequot Press

DEDICATION

To Deb, who fails with great charm to grasp any of this, yet supports my every effort.

The Lyons Press is an imprint of The Globe Pequot Press.

10 9 8 7 6 5 4 3 2 1

Designed by Compset, Inc.

10 9 8 7 6 5 4 3 2 1

Library of Congress Cataloging-in-Publication Data

Henderson, David R.

Ultimate guide to shotgunning: guns, gear, and hunting tactics for deer, big game, upland birds, waterfowl, and small game / Dave Henderson.

p. cm.

Includes index.

ISBN 1-59228-162-1 (hc : alk. paper)

1. Shotguns. 2. Hunting. I. Title.

SK274.5.H46 2003

799.2'028'34—dc21

2002156766

CONTENTS

BOOKS BY DAVID R. HENDERSON

WHITE TALES: A Modern Look at Deer Hunting

Shotgunning for Deer

Gunsmithing Shotguns

FOREWORD

A decade or so back, when I was trying to get started as a gun and hunting writer, I was invited to cover one of the NRA's Great American Hunter Tour events in the Catskill Mountains of New York. The first day there I ran into the editor of one of the big whitetail magazines, and he invited me to dinner that evening. I arrived at the restaurant to find a large man wearing the nametag "Dave Henderson," who was to join us for dinner.

I had been reading Dave's stuff for years, and I was pretty damned intimidated when I shook his hand because, in my world, this was a "made guy."

In the years since, Dave and I have shared a lot of adventures. Whether it was working as press liaisons for the shooting venue at the 1996 Olympics, bear hunting in northern British Columbia, or chasing whitetails all over the country, one thing has remained constant—something always happens to make things interesting.

We have experienced car trouble in the middle of a brewing gang fight and tents filled with toxic fumes, suffered severe weather, bad outfitters, spooky hotels, getting lost (several times), and a near car-jacking in New Orleans. We missed the bomb at Centennial Park in Atlanta by minutes and have missed plane connections by even less. One recent hunting trip actually ended with Dave shoeless.

Dave is my oldest and truest friend in this business. He is the guy I go to for advice on writing or when I need some balance for my raging temper. He may not know it, but his unique perspective on the world and this business is probably one of the biggest reasons I am still working. He is also the guy I go to any time I need advice on shotguns of any kind.

His reputation in the magazine world was built in great part on his expertise with slug guns. But that reputation also masks his skill and vast knowledge of the more traditional uses of shotguns for shooting at little targets that scurry and fly.

Beyond that, the guy can do something a lot of other gun scribes can't. He can write. I don't mean just turning in technically correct text; that is craft and it can be learned. Dave writes as an art, and that is born of talent and nurtured by passion. I remember attending a writing seminar in California some years ago. The speaker, a very good novelist, was describing a book by a new author he had just discovered: "I read the first twenty pages of this guy's brilliant prose before I slammed the book shut and yelled at the empty room, 'I suck!' "

That's how Dave often makes me—and no doubt a lot of other writers—feel about our talents.

Bryce M. Towsley

PREFACE

D avid H. Henderson is a delightful man. A true southern gentle-
man with a passion for the outdoors—particularly wielding a
fine gun over a brace of good bird dogs—and an extraordinary talent
for putting his feelings and experiences into words. That's part of the
reason that I have spent a good portion of my professional life apolo-
gizing to editors and readers for not being *that* David Henderson.
Sadly, we aren't even related. If you bought this book thinking it was
his work, I again apologize.

David H., with whom I am acquainted through the quirk of
similar appellation (I'm David R.), is a well-known North Carolina
writer who has authored four books on bird hunting and whose by-
line has, over the years, appeared in *Gun Dog, Wing and Shot*, and
Waterfowl. He is a retired lawyer, son of a judge, and a "Son of the
South." He grew up in a rich tradition, where wingshooting was an
honored pastime and where shooting birds over a good dog was a
rite of passage.

In my boyhood, if I let a grouse or pheasant fly before shooting
the elders of my clan would admonish me with a gruff order to "quit
fooling around." Our hunting time was limited, and we had to get
our grocery orders filled with expediency. When hunting with my
pubescent cronies, however, wingshooting was far more common.
Not because it was more sporting to flush the bird, but rather because the noise and bustle of shotgun-toting kids scrambling to out-
gun each other had a tendency to unnerve sitting birds.

I was probably in my forties before I ever shot a flying bird with
a gun that had two barrels. The first time I showed up at a sporting
clays course, dressed in cut-offs and a T-shirt, the assembled gunners
looked at me as if I were a character out of a Dickens novel. "Gee, a

flintlock!" remarked one of the more witty patrons upon seeing the battered Browning Auto-5 in the crook of my arm.

I shot my first whitetail in the early 1960s with a single-shot 20 gauge, and shortly before this book was finished I took my ninetieth deer with a slug and a rifled-barrel 12-gauge shotgun that bore virtually no resemblance to that ancient single-shot.

These facts are not offered as confessions but as an explanation of who wrote this book and where he came from. On the positive side, in nearly 40 years of shotgunning, I've passionately hunted marmots, cottontail, snowshoe, and jackrabbits, several varieties of squirrels and upland birds, crows, doves, waterfowl, turkeys, whitetail deer, bears, boars, pronghorns, caribou, and even a plains bison.

While I admire fine shotguns, I don't own any. There are a couple of fairly handsome doubles in my safes, but they earned their positions more for their fit than their finish. I'm not a collector or fancier, have never paid more for a shotgun than a pickup truck—and I've been known to drive some pretty ratty pickups. Guns are, quite simply, tools in my life. Those that fit comfortably and perform correctly are well used and cared for; anything else merely passes through the shop and into other hands.

I've developed into a pretty fair wingshot primarily because I love to shoot and claybird games offer far more opportunity than the seasonal flights of the feathered variety. I've written two previous books on shotgunning and countless articles, which have allowed me to develop friendships with some of the best shotgun minds of my generation. The late ATA Hall of Famer Frank Little, who may well have been the best there ever was with a trap gun in his hands, was a great friend. World-class shooting instructor Steve Schultz is both a mentor and a buddy.

I've also been privileged to hang with the best gun writers of this era. It means a great deal to me that my good friend and one of the best technical minds in the business, Bryce Towsley, wrote the foreword for this book. I've been close enough to learn from and trade ideas and theories with legendary shotgun gurus like Don Zutz and Nick Sisley and have picked up knowledge from the likes of Jim Carmichel, Layne Simpson, Bob Brister, Michael McIntosh, and John Taylor.

I've also benefited greatly from working with Darren Brown, the editor who gave shape, direction, and coherence to this work.

This book is thus a comprehensive look at what shotguns are and what they were and what they can and can't do and why. I've spent most of my adult life getting paid to do things most sensible men would gladly pay for. This book is simply an extension of that good fortune and I'm grateful for the opportunity to share it with you.

Dave Henderson
December 2002

INTRODUCTION
A BRIEF HISTORY

" **T** he real way not to miss crossing game on the wing or running, is not only to swing forward, but even more, to avoid involuntarily stopping your swing at the moment of pulling the trigger, as do most unskilled shots; because then the hand stops swinging to fire and in that instant, however brief, the bird, which does not stop, passes the line of aim and is missed behind. It is essential to accustom the hand to follow the game without stopping."

Shotgunning has a long tradition.

What well could be a run-on sentence excerpted from a modern wingshooting instruction manual is actually advice from Frenchman Magne de Marolles, written about 1740.

This most basic tenet of wingshooting may well have been a commonly known fact even back then—or maybe not. The history of the shotgun, you see, is a cloudy one. We can't even pinpoint the birth of the shotgun since virtually all early shoulder-shot firearms could be loaded with either shot or a single ball. What was a shotgun and what was a musket?

The late Don Zutz, as practical a shotgun mind as ever visited a skeet field or goose blind, maintained that shotgun history should start with wingshooting—a pastime devoted solely to shotgunning.

The Zutz logic further held that wingshooting itself wasn't really practical until the invention of percussion ignition in 1806, since the lag time in the flintlock's *pfitz-whoosh-boom!* cycle of ignition allowed for so much flight time that hitting anything on the wing was hardly worth the effort. Factor in the obstacles faced when hunting prey such as waterfowl with an open flashpan in inclement weather and the idea of wingshooting with a flintlock looks absolutely ludicrous.

But Zutz was also an historian, and he effectively discounted his own theory on the dawn of shotgunning by finding references to wingshooting throughout sixteenth- and seventeenth-century literature. The earliest word, in fact, came as much as three centuries before Alexander Forsythe, a clergyman and waterfowler, developed the concept of percussion ignition in England. Early shooters apparently didn't know how difficult wingshooting was with a flintlock simply because they'd never had anything else.

Thus, it looks like the history of shotgunning as we know it started somewhere in the early 1500s. The introduction of chlorate of potassium and fulminate of mercury in a small cup ignited by a

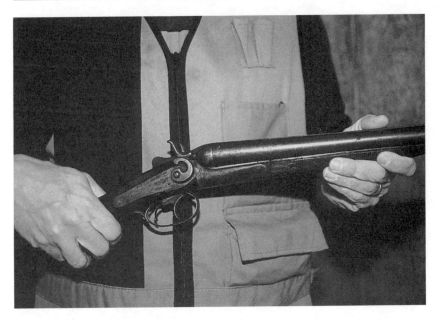

A double-hammer sidelock shotgun made in the late 1890s.

hammer blow certainly changed the course of shotgunning, but it didn't initiate it.

In fact, Englishman Joseph Manton may have been just as significant as Forsythe in the development of shotgunning since it was his early 19th-century design of the double-barreled gun that earned him the legacy "Father of the Modern Shotgun." Manton's design has not been changed appreciably since 1880.

On these shores, the Parker brothers, the Remington family, the Bakers, the Smiths in Ithaca, and the Olins and Mossbergs subsequently made marks of their own in shotgun history.

1

THE SHOTGUN

GAUGE DEFINED

Today's shotguns are measured by the gauge system rather than calibers. Historically, the term "gauge" referred to the number of equal-sized balls cast from one pound of lead that would pass through a barrel of specific diameter. The 12-gauge's bore would allow a dozen balls of equal size to pass through, the 20-gauge 20 balls, and so forth. The 16-gauge is the classic example since that gauge would accommodate 16 one-ounce lead balls. Shotgun manufacturers still refer to gauges in their models, but they use decimal measurements to identify choke constrictions.

According to the Sporting Arms and Ammunition Manufacturers Institute (SAAMI), the following are nominal bore diameters: 10-gauge 0.775 inches; 12-gauge 0.729; 16-gauge 0.665; 20-gauge 0.615; 28-gauge 0.550; and .410-gauge 0.410. Obsolete gauges that remain in SAAMI specifications include the 4-gauge (1.052 inches), 6-gauge (0.919) and 8-gauge (0.835). I've also seen 24-gauge (0.579), 32-gauge (0.526), and 36-gauge (0.506) guns, which have been relegated to wallhanger status by the lack of suitable loads.

As stated in the NRA's *Firearms Fact Book*, the system of expressing shotgun bore sizes by gauge rather than by decimal or

The Marlin 55 goose gun is a stalwart in the company's product line—and its 36-inch barrel is the longest currently available.

metric measurements is—like many things related to smoothbores—a matter of tradition. All of the modern gauges are identified by normal measurements, except the runt of the litter, the .410-gauge, which is labeled by its bore diameter.

One explanation may be that the English numbered gauge system's smallest gauge was 50, which measured 0.453 inch. Presumably, anything smaller needed to be labeled by diameter. (That saves us from going squirrel hunting with a 67½-gauge.)

Letter gauges were at one time used for some very large bore sizes, with "A" the largest at a 2-inch diameter, "B" 1.938, on down to "P" at 1.250 inches.

The largest gauge common today is the 10. Manufacturers originally chambered this gauge for 2⅞-inch shells, but the current chambers are 3½ inches. Today the 10-gauge is a specialty gun used by goose and turkey hunters and those who chase deer with buckshot—all seeking to put as many pellets as possible in their patterns. The only guns currently chambered for 10-gauge are the Browning BPS pump, H&R (New England Firearms) single-shot, Remington SP-10 (successor to the Ithaca Mag-10) and Browning Gold autoloaders.

The advent of the 3½-inch 12-gauge has put the demand for 10-gauge in decline. The 12 is the world's most popular gauge since it can handle anything from very light to very heavy loads in 2¾-, 3-, and 3½-inch chambers.

In lighter shotguns, the popularity of the 0.615-inch bore 20-gauge made it a sensible alternative to the heavier, harder-recoiling 12. The in-between 16-gauge was mostly phased out in the 1980s. The 20 is a common choice among upland bird hunters seeking a physically lighter gun to tote on long days afield. It is one of the four gauges in skeet competition, and with its ⅞- and 1-ounce loads, it is effective on small game. There are 3-inch 20-gauge loads and chambers available, but most aren't conducive to good patterning.

The 0.550-inch 28-gauge may be the most useful of the small bores due to its comfortable size and effective ¾-ounce payload, but its use is primarily limited to bird hunting. While it is also a popular skeet gauge, the 28 is often overlooked in favor of the more powerful 20 in the field.

The .410, another skeet gauge, is pretty much limited to shooting small vermin due to its tiny payload. The exceptions would be found among dedicated upland bird hunters shooting in specific situations and youngsters heading to the squirrel woods.

Actually, the gauge system was continued for rifles in gauges up to No. 1 (1.669 inches) until the middle of the twentieth century and is still correct—although rarely used—for smoothbores intended to shoot a single bullet. The system was abandoned when rifle bullets became increasingly elongated, making bore size a less meaningful indication of the weight of the bullet.

It wasn't until the 1840s that tool making and gauging techniques were precise enough to measure gun bores with anything like the accuracy that we see today. It was, however, always practical to classify bores by the approximate weight of the ball they took, although this didn't signify a precise specification of bore diameter. The present standard bore diameters, though specified on the old rule, became possible only with the ability to make accurate measurements.

CHOOSE YOUR ACTION

There are essentially five types of actions in modern shotguns: double barrels, pumps, autoloaders, and bolt actions or single shots. Each type comes with advantages and disadvantages.

THE DOUBLE GUN

The doubles are the most romantic and personal shotguns. These so-called "twice guns" are light and easy to point and carry—classic wingshooting instruments. The side-by-side doubles, over the latter part of the twentieth century, gave way in popularity to the over-under. The over-under aims like a rifle, which in America—a nation of riflemen—may be part of its appeal.

The most popular version in both side-by-side and over-under doubles is the boxlock, an action devised late in the nineteenth century that carries the trigger(s), sears, hammers, and attendant springs within the action body. The alternative is the sidelock, which carries the sear, hammer, mainspring, and tumbler on plates mounted on the sides of the action, inletted into the head of the stock and action bar. The sidelock is a holdover from the days of flintlock and percussion-lock shotguns. The average sidelock had ten or more individual parts, while the modern boxlock uses just four.

Most modern side-by-sides are boxlocks, which are more bulky but also more durable. High-dollar British guns like Purdey and

Holland & Holland still use sidelock actions. A quality sidelock generally offers better trigger pulls than a boxlock and offers the added safety advantage of interceptor sears.

Two-barrel shotguns—whether side-by-side or over-under—offer an instant choice between two chokes and, in all but the lowest grades, excellent between-the-hands balance. Some shooters also prefer the tang safety, which is worked by the thumb of the shooting hand.

Double guns are used almost exclusively by bird hunters. You won't find many deer hunters shooting doubles—with the possible exception of a tradition-bound Old South dog hunter using buckshot—because barrels on double guns usually have different points of aim, and a deer gun is aimed rather than pointed as in wingshooting.

The hunter using a double gun will likely find that all but the most expensive guns today use ejectors rather than extractors (meaning spent hulls are jettisoned automatically when the gun is broken

Remington's 3200 is one of the few American-made double barrels on the market today.

open), and the dainty "splinter" forends have, for the most part, been replaced by wider, bulkier versions on many modern guns.

The drawbacks to doubles are their expense and limited firepower, just one step above the hapless single shot. Ithaca, Winchester, Fox, Parker, and Remington made classic American side-by-side doubles, but the Ruger Gold Label is the only American-made production side-by-side today. Weatherby offers one made offshore, as does Beretta and a variety of European gunmakers. Prices range from $300 for a Cowboy Action-Darling Stoeger Coach Gun to $30,000 and more for a high-grade Winchester, Fox, or Ithaca "reproduction."

Ruger and Remington make the only over-unders produced on these shores, but stack-barrel models built offshore are available through Browning, Winchester, Weatherby, Beretta, Charles Daly, Fabarms and others.

THE PUMP ACTION

The pump is the quintessential American action. It became extremely popular in the middle of the twentieth century when doubles priced themselves out of the general marketplace and the hunting gun market soared in the wake of World War II.

The pump has been the most popular style of repeating shotgun ever since. It has a single barrel over a tubular magazine and the action operates by pulling the forend rearward on a rail to trigger the ejection of the spent hull. Pushing the forend forward feeds a new shell from the magazine to the chamber and locks the breechbolt back to battery, ready for the next shot.

Classic American pumps include the Winchester Model 12 and exposed-hammer Models 1897 and 97, the Ithaca 37 and Browning BPS, and the Remington Models 31 and 870, the latter still a bestseller (with nearly 10 million already in circulation).

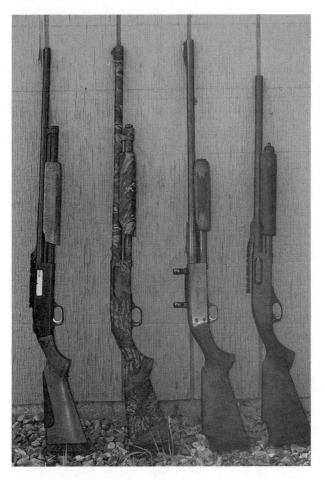

The pump-action shotgun is popular because it is inexpensive, durable, and simple.

The pump action offers simplicity, durability, low price, and a lighter weight, but you will likely pay for those advantages with heavier recoil. The compact, lightweight aspect of the pump makes it the darling of the deer stalker and upland bird hunter, and its quick, simple action attracts waterfowlers who ply their trade in elements that can foul up more sophisticated actions. Follow-up shots are easier with a pump than with any action other than an autoloader, but again, heavier recoil results from the light, compact design. Some pumps (like Mossbergs) have the safety on the rear slope of the receiver, others on the trigger guard.

Remington 12-, 16-, and 20-gauge 870s and the 12-gauge Mossberg 500 and 835 Ultri-Mag are among the international sales leaders every year. Ithaca's M37 pump comes in 12-, 16-, and 20-gauge specialty configurations for deer hunters, waterfowlers, turkey hunters, small game and bird hunters, and claybird shooters. They range from a sub-6-pound, 20-gauge featherweight to the 11-pound, 12-gauge, bull-barreled DeerSlayer III, which is available only by special order.

Pumps can range from $200 for a smoothbore Blue Light Special to $600–$800 for the true specialty guns.

THE AUTOLOADER

Want to tame recoil? Your best bet is the autoloader, which uses either a mechanical system or a gas piston to suppress the kick. The autoloader is also the quickest repeating action, firing a round, ejecting the spent hull, and replacing it in the chamber with a loaded one on each trip of the trigger. The Browning Auto-5, made from 1905 to 1997 (also the Remington Model 11 and Savage Model 720 under the same patent), is an American classic autoloader.

The drawbacks are that autoloaders are the heaviest shotguns made and the most expensive — barring high-end double guns. They are also more complicated, often less reliable (particularly in tough field conditions), and somewhat less accurate in slug shooting due to the excessive vibration caused by the cycling action.

The Remington 1100 is the lightest and oldest autoloading model on the market; it is available in 12-, 20-, 16-, and 28-gauge. Its successor, the 12- and 20-gauge 11–87, features an advanced gas-operated system in a heavier frame and optional 3½-inch chamber and comes in specialty versions for deer, turkey, and wa-

The autoloader is the heaviest and most expensive action, but it handles recoil better than any other.

terfowl hunters. Browning's Gold (and its twin, the Winchester Super-X2), Benelli's 12-gauge Super Black Eagle and M1, and Beretta's 12-gauge ES100 (formerly the Pintail and a more austere twin of the Benelli Super Black Eagle) are also popular, while Charles Daly, Fabarms, and several other European actions are also available on the U.S. market.

Autoloaders range in price from $600 to $1,200.

THE BOLT ACTION

The bolt action is inexpensive, simple, and durable, but cycling the gun is cumbersome to the point of being useless for anything other than deer or turkey hunting, where single shots are the norm. Today, the bolt action is the state of the art in slug guns. Once the least expensive, simplest shotgun action, the addition of the rifled barrel and a few other amenities (like fiber-optic sights, rifle-style synthetic

The bolt-actions and single-shots are the simplest actions available on a shotgun.

stocks, and scope mounts) has turned the bolt from a beginner's gun into the most inherently accurate slug gun available.

Mossberg, Savage, and Marlin make the only production bolt–action shotguns today. Marlin's Model 55 goose gun, with its 36-inch, 12-gauge barrel, is unique. The Maverick model of the Mossberg line also offers a lower-priced bolt, smoothbore version of the parent firm's 695 slug gun. Bolt-action guns are priced between $225 and $400.

THE SINGLE SHOT

Single shots are by far the simplest, least expensive shotgun actions. They also kick harder than any other gun, and follow-up shots are problematical at best.

Single-shot, break-open guns are built by H&R and New England Firearms, Mossberg, and Thompson Center. H&R and New

England Firearms, which are now owned by Marlin, offer entry-level and specialty single-shot guns that range in price from less than $100 in the Tracker version to the $300 12- and 10-gauge turkey models. Mossberg's SS1-One is actually an interchangeable barrel design, as is the TC Encore, both selling for more than $400.

Virtually all pump and autoloading shotguns are available with a raised rib on the barrel and at least a single bead sight, or with an optional rifle-sighted slug-shooting version. Modern bolt-action and single-shot guns will not feature raised ribs since they are essentially slug or turkey guns that require rifle sights (often fiber optic) for aiming rather than pointing.

TRUE AMERICAN DOUBLES SURVIVE

A.H. Fox, Parker Brothers, Remington, Winchester, and Ithaca Gun doubles faded to black in the 1940s due to the escalating cost of skilled labor in the face of automation. But nostalgia sells, and later there were some attempts at reproducing the classics. Remington and others brought out Parker reproductions; Marlin did a modestly priced L.C. Smith sequel; U.S. Repeating Arms kept the Winchester 21 alive; and Ithaca Gun's NID survived through its custom shops for a while.

Some true American-made "classics" still exist for those with sufficient passion and disposal income. Regrettably, they are called "reproductions," which somehow implies that they are cheap imitations. That is an unfounded and unfair perspective often prevalent in the shotgun world. What is a reproduction and what is an original shotgun is subject to some interpretation and can be further clouded by semantics.

In reality, today's reproductions are built in America by updated companies to exactly the same specs as the originals.

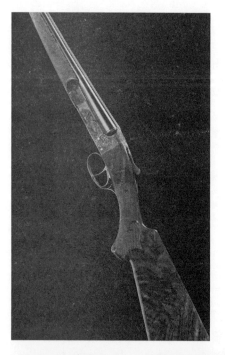

An Ithaca Classic double.

Modern metals, manufacturing methods, and finishes actually make them better than the one-offs. Honestly, aren't all American firearms built by something other than the original companies? Why aren't they called reproductions?

Fortunately, three enterprising shotgun aficionados had the vision and finances to bring back those classic guns, and they did it well, regardless of the labels. Thank Tom Skeuse, Tony Galazan, and Steve Lamboy for that rebirth. It actually started in the early 1980s when Skeuse, president of Reagent Chemical & Research, Inc., reached a station in life where he could realize a dream— bringing his favorite gun back to production. Thus Parker Reproductions were introduced at the 1984 S.H.O.T. Show.

The "Reproductions" part of the label came for strictly legal reasons. Remington, you see, has held the manufacturing rights and the use of the Parker name since the 1930s. Remington was willing to license Skeuse's manufacturing of the gun but refused to grant use of the Parker name, insisting that the Japanese-made guns be labeled reproductions. On top of that, Winchester was part owner of the Japanese manufacturing facility, so the guns officially became "Parker Reproductions by Winchester."

The guns were literal clones of America's most famous double gun. The company, however, fell victim to overseas economics in 1988, and the Skeuse family failed to find a suitable manufacturer to make quality guns at anywhere near their cost objective.

A friend of mine with a good background in both Japanese economics and American doubles tried to pick up the ball again in the 1990s, but promised development financing from his rural New York county evaporated and the new Parkers were left stranded in historical limbo.

Next, it was Connecticut double gun fancier and machine tool designer Galazan who wanted to re-create, rather than reproduce, a classic American double. He'd long admired Ansley Fox's sturdy, simple, yet exquisite design.

In the early 1990s Galazan negotiated with Savage to obtain the A.H. Fox name, but he left the 60- to 90-year-old tooling in mothballs. To resurrect those primitive machines and employ craftsmen to hand-finish the relatively sloppy results would be cost prohibitive and would have limited Galazan to a tiny shop and a handful of replicas each year. Leave that to Williamsburg.

Galazan, by working from original blueprints and by sizing critical components of several Fox originals, came up with a common size and used it to design investment casting for the production of the new A.H. Fox.

He later extended his art to include the Winchester 21 in much the same manner, following the original New Haven blueprints with exacting detail and fitting and finishing the "new" guns with the same meticulous care that Winchester craftsmen did early in the last century.

Of course, one expects to pay for such quality and attention. For example, if you prefer a "knock-around" field gun in 16- or 20-gauge, the appropriate CE Grade can be had for around $10,000. There are four escalating grades of walnut and other goodies that take models into the same retail neighborhood as luxury sedans.

Lamboy hunted with his grandfather's 28-gauge Ithaca NID in his youth and carried into adulthood a dream of resurrecting the marque that died out in 1948. A family friend, Bob Neill, had retained rights to the NID when his Ithaca Acquisition Corporation fell into bankruptcy with its Model 37 pump in 1995.

The Ithaca line came back to life as Ithaca Gun LLC in 1996, and Lamboy left a comfortable position as Realtree Camo's licensing chief, bought the NID rights, and started work on an Ithaca Classic Doubles manufacturing facility in his Victor, New York backyard at about the same time.

The new NIDs are absolutely faithful to the original blueprints and design salvaged by Neill from the old Ithaca, New York factory in the 1980s. Like Galazan, Lamboy took the average of many old NID parts, had them cast and machined in a common size, and started building guns. Although some parts are manufactured overseas, the fitting, finishing, engraving, and some manufacture is done right here. The results are several clicks past impressive.

In 2002, S. R. Lamboy & Co. Gunmakers added Grades 5E and 6E and Superlative Class guns featuring fine English scroll and 24-carat gold inlays on the receivers, reproduced from the patterns of early Ithaca custom engraver William McGraw. They are stocked with high-grade American or Turkish walnut, hand-checkered at 26 lines to the inch in the original Ithaca *fleur-de-lis* pattern. Receivers are bone and charcoal case-hardened by the incomparable Doug Turnbull, who is arguably not only one of the world's best but also Lamboy's lifelong friend and a virtual neighbor.

2

GUNFIT AND CHOOSING THE RIGHT GUN

Regardless of your choice of guns, it must fit you. That is, your gun must have the proper drop and cast to the stock so that it points exactly where you're looking as soon as it's mounted. Understand that a gun bought off a dealer's shelf is a compromise. It probably fits no one perfectly but can be used casually by virtually anyone.

But when we're talking fit, a tall person can't shoot the same gun that a short person can. Nor can someone with a round face fit the same gun as a thin-faced person. Women are built differently than men—a fact for which we're all grateful—but that means that their guns must be shaped differently to be effective.

Professional fitting, which is the best option if you are serious about wingshooting with a particular gun, will likely be available only at custom shops, wingshooting schools, or high-end dealers that have the resources not only to measure fit but also to tailor the gun to fit you. Expect to pay at least $200 for a fitting, particularly if it entails shooting a "try gun" (a gun that is adjustable for pitch, length, cast, and so forth) on the range.

If you are just getting started, or selecting a shotgun without the aid of a professional gunfit specialist, knowing the basics of gunfit will still help you find a gun that fits you fairly well.

THE BASICS OF GUNFIT

Critical stock measurements in fitting a gun to a shooter include pull, drop, pitch, and cast. Let's start with the most common bugaboo—length of pull. Pull is the distance from the front of the trigger shoe (or the front trigger on a double-trigger gun) to the center of the buttstock. Most factory guns come out of the box at 14 to 14⅜ inches length of pull. If your sleeve length is 32 inches and you commonly shoot in light clothing, this should be a decent fit.

But not everyone fits that criteria. Youth or ladies models, for example, are often in the 12- to 12½-inch range. If the stock is too

Measuring for length of pull.

short, your gun will shoot high. Also, you'll probably bang your nose with the thumb of your trigger hand, which will make you crawl around for a comfortable spot on the stock. Conversely, if the pull is too long the gun will shoot low, pose a problem in mounting, and will be a real bear when you're chasing fast crossing targets.

It is fairly easy, but by no means precise, to determine if a particular gun's length of pull is right for you. With your shooting arm extended parallel to the floor, bent upward 90 degrees at the elbow, place the butt of the gun in the crook of your elbow and see where the tip of the trigger finger lies in relation to the trigger. It may be just as easy—and equally imprecise—to see if, when the gun is mounted, the thumb of the trigger hand is sufficiently far from your nose to avoid collisions upon recoil.

A well-fitted gun will have the pitch adjusted to the shooter, but most of us simply adjust to the length of pull on our specific guns. Creeping the lead hand farther forward on the forend is a method used to artificially lengthen a gun that is slightly short.

So to adjust pull, we just shorten or lengthen the stock, right? Yes, but then you've changed the comb height, since shotgun stocks typically slope downward toward the butt. (The comb is the top of the stock where your cheek rests.) Factory field guns usually come in at 1½ inches of comb height, trap guns about ⅛-inch lower. Thus, the comb must be adjusted whenever the pull is altered.

Drop is the measurement taken at the topmost surface of a shotgun's stock that determines the elevation of the shooter's head and eye in relation to the bore. To measure drop, a straightedge is laid upon the rib or on top of the barrels and a measurement taken from the bottom of the straightedge to the top of the stock.

Drop at the comb is measured at the very front top of the comb. Drop at the face is an optional measurement taken midway between the front, top surface of the comb, and the heel. This is the point at which the shooter's face contacts the stock. Because of

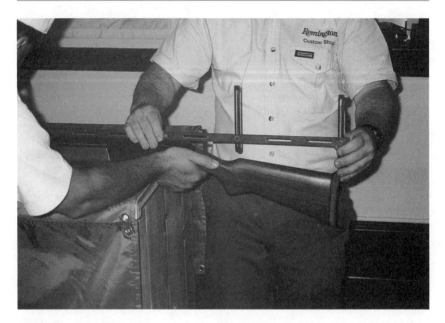

Measuring a stock for drop.

variations in exact placement, drop at the face is not often thought of as a major factor in gunfitting. Drop at the heel is measured at the farthest end of the buttstock, where the buttplace or recoil pad meets the top of the comb. It is a vital measurement in determining the placement of the shooter's head and eye on the gunstock.

Get those factors adjusted and you can fine-tune the fit by changing the gun's pitch. Pitch is the angle the stock is cut to meet the shoulder. Normal, or down, pitch is considered 2 to 2.5 inches. Pitch governs how the butt lies on the shoulder. Too little pitch will allow the toe of the stock to dig into the shoulder and also has a tendency to allow the stock to slide down and off the shoulder when fired. Too much pitch, on the other hand, makes the stock slip up into the cheek, accentuating felt recoil.

Increasing the down pitch can help heavy men and well-endowed women by making the gun easier to mount and more

Using a simple test to measure for pitch.

comfortable. Decreasing the pitch makes it easier to hit fast-rising clay and feathered birds and reduces muzzle jump.

Careful gunfitting includes studying the shape of the individual's shoulder and chest and adjusting the pitch to keep the gun comfortably in position. Women often require more pitch than men. The most common way of measuring pitch is by standing the gunbutt on the floor with the action or receiver against a squared door frame, then noting the distance (amount of pitch) from the top of the rib to the vertical doorjamb. If the muzzle and barrel are flush to the wall in this position, it's called neutral pitch. If the muzzle touches the wall with the butt squarely on the floor and the receiver is not touching, it's negative pitch. Obviously, negative pitch is very difficult to measure.

The British method of fitting entails also taking measurements from the trigger to the toe, center, and heel of the stock, providing the stocker with precise figures to use for proper adjustment of pitch.

You can also get into cast-on and cast-off if you're the type who has an affinity for an absolute custom fit. Cast-off is a lateral bend in a buttstock to compensate for the thickness of the shooter's face. Cast-off is for right-handed shooters, cast-on for lefties. In a bespoke, or custom-stocked, shotgun cast is a part of the stock from the stock's head, where it meets the action, right through the butt.

If there is no cast in the original stock of your gun it can be added by either removing wood from the cheek side of the comb or having the stock bent with heat and a bending jig. Women often need cast in a stock to fit their face and additional cast at the toe to move it away from the breast.

All stock adjustments should only be made by someone who knows the drill. A change of ⅛ inch in any critical dimension or angle can change point of impact by a foot at 40 yards.

The stock on this slug gun is cast-off at the toe.

When the gun fits you should be able to mount the gun with your eyes closed and find the rib perfectly aligned when you open them.

Okay, so the gun fits. That's a major step; now let's make it perform. If you're turkey hunting or shooting decoying waterfowl, gun balance doesn't mean much. But a well-balanced gun is very helpful in wingshooting, where correctly mounting the gun is critical to success. Ideally, 50 percent of the gun's weight is between the hands, 25 in buttstock and 25 in barrels. Shotguns for target shooting, however, have more weight forward, which tends to steady the hold and accentuate the barrel swing.

THE STOCK

If a shotgun is a tool, the stock is its handle—the part with which the shooter makes the most intimate contact. It must be sturdy and comfortable and it hurts nothing if it looks good.

Gunstocks have been carved or fabricated from a variety of substances. I've heard of stocks carved from ivory, cast from metals, molded from polymers, laid up from fiberglass and thin layers of wood; shotgun expert Michael McIntosh even talks about one laminated from buffalo horn.

Wood, of course, is the most common and successful medium for stock making, and a long list of woods have been used: birch and beech, oak and pine, ash, cherry, mesquite, myrtle, pecan, holly, teak, mahogany, madrone, persimmon, and I'm sure a few other native American woods that I've left out. African ekki, ebony, benge, bubinga, sifou, and other exotics have also been tried.

But there is a favorite. Walnut, in its many forms, reigns supreme as a medium from which to fabricate gunstocks. It is strong, durable, lightweight, and flexible. It looks and smells good, is easy to work, and takes finishes well. American black walnut is indigenous to the eastern U.S., while Claro walnut, otherwise known as California or Hinds, is found in the West.

Smaller shooters need smaller guns—not just shorter stocks. The size of the grip has a profound effect on how well a gun fits the shooter, as shown with this Youth Model Remington 1100 in the hands of a teenage girl.

Walnut is so popular that you'll also find several varieties of foreign walnut growing on these shores, as well as hybrids. Treasured exotic walnuts include Circassian, Turkish, Persian, Himalayan, Bastogne, English, French, and Spanish—each with its own distinctive color and tone, grain and feather. But American black walnut is the densest and hardest of all. It is also stiffer and doesn't flex under recoil like European walnut does.

Personal comfort and preference will dictate whether the shooter likes the look and/or feel of a straight grip or pistol-style grip. Double guns, regardless of grade, will undoubtedly feature hand-cut and probably elaborate checkering (the higher the grade, the more elaborate) on the grip and forend, while an inexpensive gun in any other action usually comes with stamped checkering or none at all.

Regardless of how it looks and feels, however, the stock is still a handle. And that handle must fit the shooter or the gun is simply a tomato stake.

3

ALL ABOUT BARRELS

W e all know that the barrel (or barrels) of a shotgun is the tube that contains and directs shot toward the target. The chamber, at the breech end, is a portion of the barrel that holds the unfired shell in position for detonation. There is a forcing cone immediately forward of the chamber—a tapered area that takes the chamber diameter gradually down to barrel diameter. Its function is to provide a smooth transition for the ejecta—wad, shot, and gas—from the chamber into the cylinder itself.

Three to seven inches from the muzzle another forcing cone starts, this one tapering from barrel diameter to choke diameter. The choke constriction shapes the shot charge. Extending the forcing cones eases the trauma on the shot charge, giving it more room for the individual pellets to sort themselves out before traversing the tube. This also reduces felt recoil and improves pellet pattern due to the decreased number of deformed pellets.

In older barrels, those made before the advent of plastic, gas-sealing wads, the chamber forcing cones are often short and abrupt—maybe ⅜ to ½ inch in length with a 5- to 7-degree taper.

Newer designs offer 1½- to 3-inch forcing cones, which provide a longer and more gentle transition for the shot column.

Backbored, or over-bored, barrels are common on custom turkey and waterfowl guns and can be found in Browning Gold and BPS and Winchester Super-X2 12-gauge guns (Invector Plus), as well as in Mossberg's 835 Ultri-Mag. A backbored barrel offers a much larger interior diameter, designed to allow an easier passage for the shot charge that results in less pellet deformity, more consistent patterning, and less felt recoil.

Backbored 12-gauge barrels commonly sport interior diameters in the 0.735 to 0.740 range. The term is often used for barrels that have longer forcing cones at the breech and muzzle as well, which serves the same purpose. Those barrels require much less constriction to get tight patterns, though.

Having counted many, many little holes in patterning targets, I can honestly say that I haven't seen any better performance from

The barrels on an over-under sit one on top of the other, allowing a comfortable sight plane.

backbored barrels than from those with extended forcing cones. In fact, gunmakers tell me that chamber forcing cones longer than three inches do not provide any additional benefit.

BARREL LENGTH

In our youth we probably all heard of at least one "Long Tom," usually a long-barreled, single-shot 12-gauge that was purported to turn a gallon bucket into door screen at 60 yards. Probably an exaggeration, but at one time the long barrels were necessary to fully burn the powders of the day and provide magnum velocity and energy. Today's smokeless powders burn in the first 18 or 19 inches of barrel, and the rest is ornamental.

Two experts in this field, Joe Morales of Rhino Chokes in Florida and Mark Bansner of Bansner's Ultimate Gunsmithing in Pennsylvania, trimmed long barrels and chronographed the charges and found that extra barrel length actually works as a brake, the additional friction of the wad against the barrel walls bleeding velocity off the charge.

Outdoor Life shooting editor Jim Carmichel, however, performed a similar test, taking two inches at a time off a long barrel and chronographing along the way, and found just the opposite—that the longer barrel provides a slightly higher velocity.

The generous standard deviation among shotshell velocities makes it difficult to make a definitive statement either way. Regardless, longer barrels are no longer in vogue. The reign of the Long Tom as king of American shotgunning passed a couple of decades ago. Long (30- to 32-inch) barrels faded in popularity in favor of shorter, lighter shotguns that were easier to tote afield and yielded surprising comparable ballistics. The move toward shorter barrels was based primarily on marketing—the performance dropped a little and the weight dropped a lot, which made them easier to sell. The long barrels weren't ineffective, they just didn't fit new lifestyles.

Sporting clays enthusiasts prefer longer barrels.

But the long barrel is making a strong comeback today, particularly among sporting clays enthusiasts who see 30-inch barrels as a bare necessity and 32- or 34-inchers as perfect. The fact remains that barrel length is an integral part of wingshooting dynamics. The longer barrel's improved sighting plane is one factor, so is the fact that powder is given more burning time in a longer barrel, which may aid velocity. But probably the biggest factor is that the inertia involved in swinging a longer barrel makes for a smoother swing and more certain follow-through. It simply improves a shooter's form. Maybe the old-timers had the right idea all along.

That being said, it also should be noted that the tightest-patterning shotguns in existence, those built for "card-shooting" that produce ragged one-hole patterns a couple of inches wide, have no forcing cones and no choke constriction at all. They are also extremely long—often in excess of 60 inches—which allows the shot charge sufficient time to sort itself out and the pellets to get in an orderly line while still in the confines of the tube. In essence, the shot string is formed before it leaves the barrel, resulting in an extremely uniform flight for all the pellets.

You'll also find that non-American shotguns normally have a true bore diameter of approximately 0.005 less than U.S. standard barrels (generally a true bore diameter of 0.725), which, of course, makes a difference when choosing a choke constriction.

English barrels are notoriously thin and whippy—0.02-inch wall thickness for 2- and 2½-inch chambers and 0.025 for 2¾-inch guns. American barrels are overbuilt up to 0.035. Belgian, German, French, and Italian barrels follow the American logic.

It should be noted that porting a barrel—having holes drilled in the barrel ahead of the muzzle—vents gases in a specific direction and tends to reduce barrel jump and felt recoil. That is part of the reason why so many specialty guns have ported barrels and why many extended choke tubes are similarly ported. Joe Morales of Rhino Chokes ports barrels well back from the muzzle with a series of up to 18 tiny holes that he says aid in increasing the velocity of certain loads.

In addition to reducing barrel jump, ports are known to grab and slow the shotcup, which helps separate it from the shot column. That keeps the shotcup-wad from blowing into the pattern and tends to shorten the shot string for better pattern density.

While porting a barrel has advantages, the sound pressure wave delivered to the shooter's face and ear is greatly increased by any compensator or porting. Extensive testing has shown that porting increases the report's noise level by at least eight decibels, which may not sound like much, but it represents an increase of 60 percent in the sound pressure magnitude. That's obviously significant.

European gunmakers long followed the British dictum that a shotgun's barrel length should be 40 times its bore diameter. That meant a 12-gauge gun with a 0.729 bore needed a 29.16-inch barrel, 30 inches being a reasonable compromise from a manufacturing perspective.

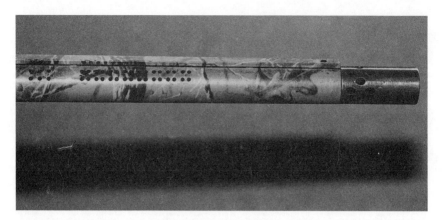

Porting helps reduce barrel jump and felt recoil, but it also has its disadvantages.

Americans, on the other hand, have long cut barrels based on comfort and use. A 26- or 28-inch barrel on a field gun—regardless of action—usually affords sufficient balance and inertia for smooth barrel swinging without being a constant hang-up in brush. Claybird shooters, however, don't worry about brush or carrying the gun and prefer the smooth-swinging characteristics (even at the sacrifice of precise balance) offered by 30- to 34-inch barrels. Turkey hunters and slug shooters who aim their guns rather than point-and-swing are perfectly happy with stubby 20- to 24-inch barrels that are easier to lug around and maneuver through brush.

IMPROVING BARREL PERFORMANCE

In recent years I've tamed barrel harmonics in my trap, turkey, and slug guns by having the barrels, and in some cases the receivers, cryogenically treated. (I also do this with muzzleloaders and rifles.) Cryogenic tempering—the deep-freezing and deep-reheating of metals—changes the molecular structure, making metal harder, and stiffer. In many cases it also makes the metal less porous, which aids in subsequent cleaning. Cryogenics have long been used to temper tools, machine parts, cutters, and, more recently, vehicle brakes, race-car components, golf clubs, softball bats, tennis rackets, and firearms barrels.

I'm not a metallurgist. In fact, I dropped out of college to join the Marines, which says something about my intellect. But I do know through personal application that cryogenic tempering has improved the performance of my guns and the guns of others. Certainly, some guns are helped more than others. With my guns, the performance difference was sometimes negligible and sometimes profoundly better. A lot depends on the initial quality of the barrel; some barrels are cut with a more meticulous, precise method or cut from metal that has already been stress-relieved and doesn't need tempering to further relieve stress.

Some friends of mine in the business are wary of cryogenics. After all, there is no visible difference in the metal after it has been treated. One friend, with a background in chemistry and metallurgy, was a scoffer. He was also an AA trapshooter who'd bought a new high-dollar gun that simply didn't shoot well, despite the fact that it had been cut to the exact dimensions of his old one. After three trips back to the factory, where he was basically told that there was nothing wrong with the gun, my friend reluctantly tried having the barrel cryogenically treated. He's right back to 100-straights, and cryogenics has a new believer.

All firearms are produced with internal stresses. As the metal is bored, reamed, and machined, mechanical stresses are created. As forgings and castings cool, the differing rates of temperature change introduce residual stresses. Even heat-treating leaves thermal stresses behind.

Careful manufacturing, of course, provides barrels that shoot well, stresses and all. Cryogenic stress relief, however, can improve even benchrest-quality barrels by relieving the internal stresses. Scatterguns do the same thing. At the end of a typical

Cryogenics can harden and stiffen a barrel, resulting in better accuracy.

10-shot trapshooting string, pattern placement can shift six inches in some shotguns. With 25 shots, pattern placement can shift up to 12 inches—a 40 percent change.

At a cost of less than $50 a cryogenic company will take a barrel down to –300 degrees Fahrenheit, hold it at that temperature for a predetermined time, then slowly bring it up through the cycle to approximately 300 degrees.

There are several cryogenic companies out there. I had 300-Below Cryogenic Tempering Services of Decatur, Illinois do my work. They tell me that their process permanently refines the grain structure of a barrel at the molecular level and produces a homogeneously stabilized barrel—whatever that is. They also say that carbon particles precipitate as carbides into a lattice structure and fill the microscopic voids. This creates a denser, smoother surface that reduces friction, heat, and wear.

4

CHOKES

In blackpowder days a shooter altered his shotgun's pattern by simply hammering the gun's muzzle slightly more closed or using a mandrel to widen it. The advent of smokeless powder shotshells, which made multiple shots quicker, easier, and more feasible, brought about more sophisticated shotgun barrels that were reamed at the muzzle to a specific diameter. The amount of constriction varied with the intended use. A wider spread to the pattern helped for short-range shooting and a denser dispersion of shot for longer shots.

Several men are credited with originating the choke system. An Illinois duck hunter by the name of Fred Kimble claimed to have invented the concept in 1867. American gunsmith Sylvester Roper received patent approval on a screw-in choke system in 1866—just six weeks before British designer William Rochester Pape filed a similar patent. Still others claim that choke systems were Spanish or French ideas. The earliest claimant on these shores appears to be Rhode Island gunsmith Jeremiah Smith, who "discovered the merits of choke boring in 1827," according to an old issue of *American Wildfowling* magazine.

Regardless, choke boring changed the face of shotgunning. The undisputed king of the choke tube is Texan Jess Briley. The

Houston machinist developed choke tubes in his garage shop in the mid-1970s and today turns out more than a million units a year under a wide variety of brand names, controlling nearly 90 percent of the market.

The nominal bore size for a 12-gauge shotgun is 0.729 inches in diameter. It is 0.779 for 10-gauge, 0.667 for 16, 0.617 for 20, and 0.550 for 28-gauge. But the choke constrictions vary slightly in designation between lead and steel (or non-toxic shot). A 12-gauge barrel with no constriction (called cylinder bore) is 0.729. A constriction of 5/1,000 inch (0.724) is considered a skeet choke for lead shooters. Improved cylinder (0.009 constriction or 0.720 diameter) for lead, however, is actually considered a skeet choke for non-toxic loads.

Conventional constriction for a 12-gauge skeet II choke is 0.012 and for modified choke it is 0.019 (or a 0.710 bore diameter). The latter is the same dimension considered improved cylinder for steel shot. Improved modified conventional choke is 0.704 (0.025 constriction), which converts to extra-full for steel shot. (See the chart at the end of this section for the generally effective ranges of each specific choke.)

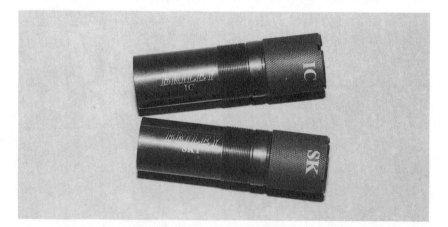

Briley is the industry's leading producer of choke tubes. The company pioneered them in the mid-1970s.

Be advised, however, that all of these measurements are specs, labels. All shotgun bores—particularly older ones—vary slightly in internal diameter, which is why a choke tube will pattern differently when screwed into different barrels. The degree of choke in a barrel is simply a measure of constriction from the bore to the muzzle. Since interior barrel dimensions can vary by as much as 20/1,000 inch from gun to gun, there is a better way of determining your choke.

The true choke size is determined by the difference between the diameter of the bore relative to the diameter of the constriction. By subtracting the diameter of the choke from that of the bore you will be able to determine the amount of constriction (choke) you have regardless of the roll-stamp on the barrel. That measurement is what really counts.

For instance, if you have a choke tube that is cylinder relative to your 0.728 bore, the choke will be modified if used in a barrel of 0.742. But if your barrel's interior diameter measures 0.732 that same choke tube would represent cylinder bore.

For another illustration, let's go back to industry specs. A full choke in conventional terms is 0.694, or a constriction of 0.035—the same dimensions considered to be a modified choke for steel. Extra-full, usually reserved for turkey hunting with lead shot, is 0.040 constriction or a 12-gauge bore diameter of 0.689.

CONSTRICTION JUST PART OF THE SYSTEM

So how does the microscopic 0.030- to 0.035-inch difference between a truly tight choke and a wide-open boring make such a marked difference in shot dispersion? Well, that tiny difference in diameter in itself doesn't make all that difference—it couldn't. The answer is that the choke is just one part of a complex system that orders pattern development.

Choke constriction does play an important role, but just as vital are a pair of dynamic forces that work in concert with the constriction to shape the shot charge before setting it free. The first factor is the pressure of the trailing wad on the base of the shot charge as it clears the muzzle, and the second is the air resistance (drag) that works against pellets once they escape the controlling wad and powder gases.

The pellets, encased in the plastic shotcup, go from a standing start in the chamber to a 1,200 feet per second (fps) mass in about 0.003 of a second. That puts a lot of pressure and momentum on the wad and pellets. The wad encounters the choke taper, which constricts it slightly—from 0.0729 down to 0.695 in a full-choked barrel. That, again, is not much. But the tight choke does pinch down on the wad, slowing it and letting the shot charge escape with little or no pressure from the wad. At the other extreme, a cylinder bore or improved cylinder choke pretty much lets the wad slide through without being bothered, meaning it can remain nestled up against the base of the shot charge. A modified choke gives the wad a slightly tighter squeeze, and an improved modified comes down almost as hard as the aforementioned full choke.

Thus, the way choke constriction slows the wad pretty much determines how the shot emerges from the muzzle, at which point it encounters air resistance. Air works harder against fast-moving objects than against slower ones, and the pellets slow abruptly during the first few feet out of the muzzle.

Pattern and shot string formation depend on how powerful that rear wad pressure is. If it's heavy, as in the case of an improved cylinder choke, the charge is virtually pancaked between the opposing forces of wad pressure and air resistance and the pellets spread outward, widening the pattern. In a full choke the wad is slowed more noticeably. The choke constriction retards the wad, and the pellet string narrows down to squeeze through the smaller opening. Pellets tend to spurt through a full choke because the narrowing is a minor obstruction. They thus escape in a longer line and, since the wad is

Briley's Companion tubes weigh the same as a 12-gauge shotshell.

delayed by the choke taper, the pellets continue on a straighter course because they are not being rammed from behind as in the case of the more open choke.

This phenomenon is more pronounced at high altitudes where air is lighter. Patterns are tighter across the board at altitude due to the reduction of the air resistance factor. In a vacuum, an improved cylinder choke would theoretically deliver 100 percent patterns due to the absence of air resistance. The pellets could travel straight ahead, their superior mass giving them the momentum to outrun the wad and its potentially disruptive impact from behind.

Choke, then, is important only as it retards (or fails to retard) the wad and in how it prepares the shot charge for its impact with air resistance.

USING MULTIPLE CHOKES

As discussed earlier, just a few thousandths of an inch difference in constriction can, for a variety of reasons, make a huge difference in pattern dispersion. The problem is that most shooting situations require different degrees of constriction. For a long time the only way to overcome the choke problem was to have more than one gun or to have another barrel or several barrels for one gun, which can be an expensive proposition. The average shooter was forced to adapt his shooting to the choke of his gun.

Choke tubes—sleeves that alter the constriction of the barrel at the muzzle—have been around in one form or another for about 150 years, but it wasn't until around the midpoint of the twentieth century that shotguns with adjustable choke systems developed a strong presence in the marketplace. The most popular was the Poly-Choke, an exterior sleeve attached at the muzzle that could be screwed to open or close the constriction.

Interchangeable chokes revolutionized shotgunning.

The Cutts Compensator found early favor with claybird shooters. It was designed by Col. Richard Cutts, U.S.M.C. Retired, to reduce the muzzle climb of the BAR and Thompson submachine gun. The design became property of the Lyman Gunsight Company in 1929. The Cutts Compensator deflected gases slightly back toward the breech to reduce felt recoil. It also featured interchangeable choke tubes that screwed into the mouth of the device. You'll probably never see one in the field, but some skeet shooters still swear by them.

Virtually all modern shotguns come with a screw-in choke tube system, but they are not universal. Manufacturers use different thread patterns and choke tube dimensions. For instance, conventional Winchester, Browning, Ithaca, H&R, NEF, Weatherby, SKB, Savage, Smith & Wesson, Churchill, most Ruger shotguns, and Mossberg 500s and 9200s use Win-Choke thread systems, while Remington and 12-gauge Charles Daly autos are threaded for Rem-Choke systems. Beretta, Benelli, and Franchi have their own Mobilchoke system. Browning and Winchester's backbored guns need Invector-Plus choke tube systems, and the Mossberg 835 Ultri-Mag has a system of its own.

CHOKE VERSUS EFFECTIVE RANGE

Choke	Ideal Range (in yards)	Effective Range (in yards)
Cylinder Bore	15–22	10–27
Skeet 1	20–27	15–32
Improved Cylinder	25–32	20–37
Skeet II	30–37	25–42
Modified	35–42	30–47
Improved Modified	40–47	35–52
Full	45–52	40–57
Extra-Full	50–57	45–62

TIPS ON CHOKE TUBES

Applying oil to the threads before screwing in any choke tube makes it much easier to remove. Shooters should also be sure that a choke tube is screwed in as tightly as possible—checking after each volley of shots—to avoid barrel damage.

Ported barrels help reduce felt recoil and improve patterns, but they also make the gun's report much louder and get dirty very fast. A ported barrel or choke tube clogged with debris quickly loses its effectiveness.

The interior ballistics of steel shot loads account for why steel leaves behind a lot of carbon residue in the barrel, and particularly in the choke tube. There are shotgun and choke tube cleaners now available that are specifically formulated to combat this problem.

Always lubricate the threads of a choke tube before inserting.

5

LOADS

Getting dusted with a few No. 8s from 80 yards away across a dove field is mildly irritating. Get the same treatment with No. 4 shot in the turkey woods and you're ready to swear out an arrest warrant. In shotgun pellets, size definitely makes a difference. The No. 8 shot that is ideal for quail, woodcock, and claybird games would be totally unsuited for pheasants or rabbits, and not even in the ballpark for turkeys or any kind of big game.

Loads should also be selected by velocity—the speed that the charge is propelled downrange. (For the sake of reference, the velocity at the muzzle is used for comparison.) Muzzle velocities of less than 1,000 feet per second, for instance, are suitable for skeet and close-flushing game, while slightly higher speeds of 1,150 to 1,200 fps are better for trap and wider-flushing game. Loads for bigger game, such as turkeys, waterfowl, and varmints, should be 1,250 to 1,300 fps. Steel shot is a totally different animal and needs velocities in the 1,300 to 1,450 range in order to assure sufficient energy, given its lesser relative density, to kill efficiently.

Rifled slugs for big game are launched at 1,300 to 1,500 fps, and some conventional sabots generally fall into the 1,250 to 1,450 range. Any faster and the slugs are either deformed at setback or

Hevi-Shot, a tungsten-alloy load from Remington, is popular with turkey and waterfowl hunters.

their lead "flows" in flight and sabot halves are shed irregularly. High-velocity sabots can withstand velocities of 1,650 to 2,000 fps because of their jacketed, bullet-like designs.

Again, the velocity figures are for comparison only. The velocities noted on shell boxes and in catalogs are taken under ideal conditions—controlled environment tunnels at temperatures of 65 to 70 degrees with tight, 30-inch, 12-gauge barrels. Your velocity from a windswept, icy duck blind with a 25-inch ported barrel isn't likely to approach what is printed on the box.

Another part of the current labeling system for shell boxes is the "dram equivalent" that came into being years ago when shotshells were still loaded with blackpowder. For instance, a box labeled 3¼-1⅛-8 contained shells loaded with 3¼ drams of blackpowder and 1⅛ ounce of No. 8 shot. Blackpowder is now obsolete, yet the labeling process remains.

Today, shotshells are loaded with smokeless powder and boxes are marked to show what a given charge is equivalent to in the old blackpowder dram rating. It's done for size comparison; nothing else. But remember, smokeless powder is measured in grains, and a very small amount is equal to a much heavier charge of blackpowder. To load a shell with 3¼ drams of smokeless powder would be catastrophic.

HOW FAR?

The shot charge from a 12-gauge target load will drop to earth within 200 yards; larger pellets and more powerful loads will carry 300 yards, but the maximum effective range of any shotgun firing lead shot is 65 yards; 50 for steel, 80 for tungsten.

We've all heard about, or sometimes experienced, killing shots at longer distances. But those distances are often exaggerated or the hits were influenced far more by luck than ballistics. In my experience, the average shotgunner shouldn't attempt any shot much longer than 45 yards.

Wind deflects flying objects, and the degree to which this occurs varies with wind speed and the size, shape, density, and velocity of the object. Shot charges are not exempt, even though wind deflection is not nearly the problem that it is with a solid projectile at longer ranges. However, significant drift can occur at 40 yards and beyond under sufficient conditions. An example provided by Winchester/Olin shows that a 10-mph crosswind will deflect 1,200 fps, No. 4 lead pellets 6.56 inches off point of aim at 40 yards, 10.38 inches off at 50, 15.06 inches at 60 yards, 20.71 inches at 70, and well over two feet at 80 yards.

No. 4 steel, which is much lighter, is blown 8.36 inches off target under the same conditions at 40 yards, 13.21 inches off at 50 yards, and 19.28 inches off point of aim at 60 yards. If you're shooting steel at 70 yards—and I'd question why—you can expect 26.80 inches of deflection, with just about a yard of deflection at 80 yards.

Hunters visiting a clays course don't need heavy loads.

UPLAND BIRD LOADS

A variety of loads will work perfectly well for many upland bird species. Lead pellets are still the norm across North America, but some federally-managed wildlife areas may require non-toxic shot, even for pheasants and other upland species. Know the regulations before you shoot.

I prefer No. 6s for pheasants when hunting over dogs and No. 4s when walking cover without dogs or late in the season, when the birds are likely to run and flush long. As to gauge, anything larger than .410 will work, with 12- and 20-gauges the most popular.

When shooting flushing quail or darting doves, a much lighter load, regardless of gauge, is appropriate—usually No. 7½s or 8s. I'm similarly comfortable with 7½s for grouse and woodcock in thickets where branches and leaves can eat up wide-spreading patterns.

Dove shooters use light loads and quick-opening chokes.

For Western, open-country birds like Hungarian partridge and sharp-tailed grouse, 7½s or even 6s are good choices. Shooting sage grouse, the largest grouse in North America, calls for shot on the heavier side, while chukar and smaller Western quail species are easily brought down with 7½s.

Gauges 12 through 28 are used regularly on all upland birds, and you'll see doubles, pumpguns, and autoloaders in the hands of most bird hunters. Lighter guns are often preferable when trudging through fields for hours at a time, and many experienced shooters swear by a light little 28-gauge, although 12- and 20-gauge guns are still the most common.

SMALL GAME LOADS

Loads for small game such as rabbits and squirrels are invariably lead and relatively small and light because it doesn't take a lot of energy to perforate small critters. Mammals larger than squirrels call for field loads of No. 4, 5, or 6 shot in virtually any gauge. Many youngsters have learned small game hunting with a .410 with No. 8 or 9 shot, which is entirely adequate for squirrels. In fact, adults may prefer this small bore and its attendant light weight for walk-up squirrel hunting, where the barrel is always pointed skyward and the gun generally held at port-arms for extended periods of time.

A 20- or 28-gauge gun is plenty for hunting rabbits, either over dogs or simply walking hedgerows. Again, larger pellets are needed here because the shots are apt to be longer and are usually at running targets, where a widening pattern is an advantage.

Loads for big varmints like coyotes, foxes, and, in the West, javalinas should be no smaller than No. 4 in 12-gauge—and should only be used when calling animals to close range. No. 2s would be a better all-around choice, particularly if the shots are apt to be 30 yards or more. For marmots and other small vermin, No. 4 and No. 6 are good choices.

While small game like squirrels and rabbits only require small shot, slugs can be a great varmint round, particularly when the shots are longer.

The type of action and gauge used for small game is almost totally a personal choice. To my mind, the heft, balance, and performance of a 16-gauge double make it the perfect field gun for small game and upland birds, but the 12-gauge double and/or autoloader is not out of place. The 20 and 28 are both reliable for all but far-off critters.

Bolt-action and single-shot guns are not good choices for upland hunting and are generally relegated to turkey hunting where the gun is aimed rather than pointed and where there is less need for quick follow-ups.

MAXIMUM PRACTICAL HUNTING RANGES

Shot Size	Muzzle Velocity	Hunting Range
No. 2 shot, 1⅜ oz.	1,260 fps	55 yards
No. 4 shot, 1¼ oz.	1,330 fps	50 yards
No. 6 shot, 1⅛ oz.	1,165 fps	45 yards
No. 7½ shot, 1 oz.	1,165 fps	40 yards
No. 9 shot, ⅞ oz.	1,135 fps	35 yards

SHOT SIZES (IN INCHES)

Buckshot	Lead Shot	Steel Shot
000 buck, 0.360	No. 2, 0.150	F shot, 0.220
00 buck, 0.330	No. 4, 0.130	T shot, 0.200
0 buck, 0.320	No. 5, 0.120	BBB shot, 0.190
No. 1 buckshot, 0.300	No. 6, 0.110	BB shot, 0.180
No. 2 buckshot, 0.270	No. 7½, 0.095	No. 1, 0.160
No. 3 buckshot, 0.250	No. 8, 0.090	No. 2, 0.150
No. 4 buckshot, 0.240	No. 8½, 0.090	No. 3, 0.140
	No. 9, 0.080	No. 4, 0.130
	No. 12, 0.050	No. 5, 0.120
		No. 6, 0.110

STORING AMMUNITION

Despite what you've seen in the movies, stocks of firearm ammunition will not mass explode. According to the Sporting Arms and

Ammunition Manufacturers Institute (SAAMI), if a single cartridge or shotshell in a carton or case is caused to fire, it will not cause other or adjacent cartridges or shotshells to explode in a sympathetic or simultaneous manner.

Firearm ammunition is simply not an overly sensitive item. Ammunition will not explode due to shock or excessive vibration and, if somehow discharged in the open without the support provided by a firearm's chamber or other close confinement, it does so very inefficiently.

If a cartridge explodes outside the chamber, the projectile or debris particles from the case or hull have an extremely limited velocity and range. The only types of debris likely to be flung far are pieces of the primer cap, which may be propelled a short range—usually under 50 feet.

6

PATTERNING

Once the shot charge leaves the barrel it spreads to varying degrees, depending on the choke, barrel configuration, distance, and type and size of the pellet. The manner in which it spreads is your pattern. Your shotgun's pattern is its signature. How that particular barrel and choke combination throws a specific load at a specific distance is a dynamic and variable feature unique to that gun. Change chokes or loads and the pattern changes.

While it is essential to know where and how your gun throws a specific load, if you're hunting it is also an ethical imperative. You owe it to the prey you pursue—whether deer, turkey, other gamebirds, or small game—to know your gun's abilities and limitations. You absolutely must know where that shot charge is going when you trip the trigger. Wounding an animal should not be the result of your ignorance of the firearm and how it shoots.

Patterning techniques vary with the application. In the section of this book devoted to turkey hunting, for example, we outline a technique for patterning turkey loads—extremely full-choked, dense patterns fired from a stationary barrel aimed like a rifle at a standing bird's head and neck. You don't shoot doves, waterfowl, woodcock, or clay birds like that. Wingshooting is a whole different world. You look for consistent, wide, and well-distributed patterns at varying distances—sort of a flak screen designed to cut the margin of error when throwing a shot charge at a flying target.

BIGGER BORE, BIGGER PATTERN?

A common misconception among shotgunners is that a larger gauge throws a larger pattern. After all, it's easier to score in skeet or trap with a 12-gauge than with a 20. But while it's easier to break birds with the larger gauge, that is not because of the size of the pattern.

The rate of shot spread is controlled by the choke and other factors, not by the bore diameter. Theoretically, the pattern is about the same size whether it's a 12-, 16-, 20-, or 28-gauge. In actual use, you'll probably score higher—and find the pattern marginally wider—with the big bore because there are more pellets in the shot string and more will be deformed and/or pressured outward. This swells the pattern diameter a bit, but it doesn't really make much of a difference in the size of the pattern.

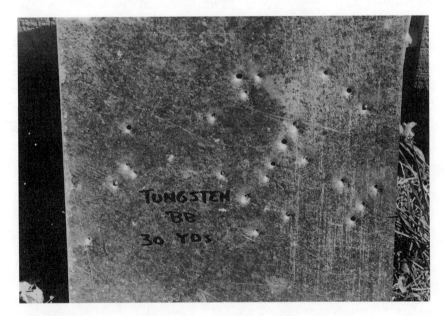

The pattern is your gun's signature.

Wingshooters look for a consistent, full pattern that covers the target well.

A trapshooter shooting from the 16-yard line, for instance, can count on a 12-inch pattern from a full-choke gun, or 16 inches from a modified barrel, regardless of gauge. At 27 yards, the full choke patterns about 24 inches in diameter and the modified 28 inches, regardless of whether the gauge is 12 or 28.

POINT OF IMPACT

Most modern raised-rib shotguns, regardless of action, center their patterns a bit high, usually 4 to 8 inches above the line of sight at 40 yards. Trap guns are aligned to print 6 to 12 inches high at that distance because the trap targets are always rising. Exceptions would be pumps, bolts, and autoloaders made for turkey and deer hunting. Since those guns are designed to be aimed rather than pointed, their stocks and sight systems are configured to allow them to shoot straight-on.

Side-by-side doubles have more flexible barrels and often throw their patterns a bit low. But don't take that as gospel without checking it at the range. Winchester regulated its classic Model 21 to shoot slightly low, but in 1960, for reasons that stayed in the boardroom, it changed its mind and moved the point of impact to dead-on. Over-unders, because the effect of gravity stiffens the barrels that sit one on top of the other, usually shoot slightly higher.

BASIC PATTERNING

It is essential to test your shotgun on a patterning board with the types of loads you'll use in the field. Some folks and shooting clubs use a whitewashed steel or iron plate for this. Lead pellets hitting the surface leave distinctive marks that can be "erased" by rolling another layer of paint over the pattern, ready for the next shot. This type of board should only be used with soft lead shot, however. Steel and other hard shot can ricochet.

Any safe backdrop that will accommodate a 40 × 40-inch sheet of paper will do as a patterning board (two strips of wide butcher paper taped together work fine). In fact, this set-up is more useful than the steel plate because pellet counts can be determined away from the range, at a table where comparisons can be made shot-to-shot.

I like to pattern new guns with an initial shot from a solid rest on a bench at 15 yards to determine if the gun shoots where it is aimed. This only tells you the alignment of the barrel-choke partnership. Follow that with an offhand shot from the same distance, since the gun will likely shoot to a different point of aim from your shoulder than from the bench.

Most bespoke (custom-made guns, usually doubles) still use fixed chokes. A highly experienced barrel borer regulates them to a specific shot size, weight, and velocity. Chances are, your Wal-Mart 870 pump is built to less stringent standards and will accept a wider variety of loads, printing some well and others not so well. Production guns today, particularly less expensive models, don't always shoot straight.

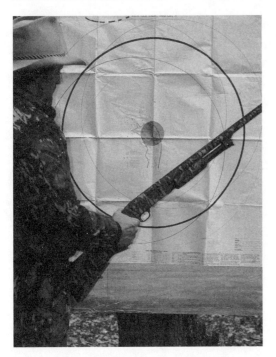

A large sheet of paper is needed as a patterning backdrop at longer ranges.

I had an over-under field gun that fit me well and was a joy to shoot, but the top barrel patterned distinctly off-center to the left. I sent it to Joe Morales at Rhino Chokes to determine if it was fixable, and the affable son of Cuban immigrants replied that he had "good news and bad news." The bad news was that he could find nothing wrong with the barrel. The good news was that the screw-in choke had been milled slightly off-center. A simple replacement choke tube fixed the problem.

Once you've determined where your gun shoots, examine how it shoots. The industry standard is a target set at 40 yards with a 30-inch circle at the center. The number of pellets your pattern throws within the circle determines the efficiency percentage of your pattern. For example, an 80-percent pattern means that 8 out of every 10 pellets in that particular load fell within that circle at that distance. The industry standard pattern percentage for a full choke is 60 to 70 percent; for modified, 55 to 60 percent; and improved cylinder is supposed to put 45 percent of its pellets (in an optimum load) in that 30-inch circle at 40 yards.

You'll find that different load sizes and pellet sizes will pattern differently out of the same choke. It all has to do with the dynamics of barrel and choke, which were discussed earlier in this book. When patterning your gun and load, don't base your judgment on one or two shots. You'll need at least 10 shots to get an approximate idea of where and how your gun is patterning.

In fact, when I've tested various loads industry experts have told me that it takes at least 100 patterns to get an accurate assessment (more than 95 percent surety) of a particular gun-load combination. For the field, however, you and I don't need that kind of efficiency—or the shoulder bruising and expense.

There are, believe it or not, scientific methods of thorough pattern reading. I know of only a couple of shooters sufficiently obsessed to utilize such means in patterning their guns. Oh, they are good shooters; very good, in fact, but strange people. I've heard the Berlin-Wanasse and Thompson-Oberfell methods discussed, but I have never tried them because there are far less elaborate ways to determine the efficiency of your pattern.

The late Don Zutz used to preach the importance of the "annular ring," a donut drawn around the core but inside the confines of the 30-inch circle. First, understand that experts look for two different pellet distributions in any pattern: the core or center of the dispersion (usually 20 inches in diameter) and the annular ring, which is a 5-inch-wide strip surrounding the core.

Why is the annular ring so important? Even the best shots aren't going to center every target, and having sufficient pellets consistently in the annular ring simply expands your efficiency and margin of error.

Patterning at various distances gives you a better idea of the true capability of your gun and load.

Not all chokes and loads are efficient at the "useable" fringes of the pattern, even if they throw a dense core pattern. The tendency toward high core density is increased by such things as harder (high-antimony) lead shot that withstands pellet-deforming setback pressures; copper or nickel-plated shot; or steel, tungsten, and other exotics. This occurs because the sturdier pellets remain round and thus fly straighter to the core of the target. Even open-bored chokes—cylinder bore, skeet, and improved cylinder—can hammer the core with hard pellets without filling in the annular ring efficiently.

To be efficient, a pattern must spread sufficiently into that annular ring. Period.

The standard 30-inch circle at 40 yards is not always the most practical way to assess a pattern. It's better to determine your own average shooting range for the game you'll be pursuing and then test over that distance. A trapshooter, for instance, wants to pattern at 32 to 35 yards for 16-yard events and at 40 yards for optimum handicap distances. Skeet shooters are better off patterning at 17 to 20 yards because most shoot their birds before they reach the NSSA distance of 21 yards at midfield. Your average shot at woodcock or quail may be 15 yards, at pheasants 25 yards, but a goose hunter or turkey hunter may want to know his pattern at 50 yards.

Patterning at your specified distance tells you much more than the 30-inch, 40-yard standard. Shoot at a specified aiming point, but don't draw the circles until after the shot. Then draw the appropriate circles around the area of greatest density. This is done because shotguns are not accurate enough to center their patterns in pre-drawn circles.

Again, the point of emphasis is that annular ring. Your goal should be to find the load that puts the most pellets in that ring and spreads them most consistently over the area.

Patterning will let you know if you have a shotgun that doesn't shoot to point of aim. Optics can be used to fix the problem for hunting turkeys and big game.

How many pellets is enough? It depends on whom you ask. But Don Zutz's estimation is that three pellets were needed in every area of the target that can be covered with a clay bird, since they are about the size of the vital area of most gamebirds. More is better, but three pellets should be sufficient.

IMPORTANCE OF THE SHOT STRING

After this serious look at pattern reading, I must bring up a point that you shouldn't believe everything you see on paper. (And as a journalist of more than 30 years experience, I feel thoroughly qualified to make that statement.) This includes the patterns we've been pouring over and analyzing for the last few pages. Yes, reading the shot dispersion is important; very important, since it establishes a reference point for determining the efficiency of your gun and load. But a paper pattern is simply a record of where the pellets end up in relation to each other on a stationary target. Chances are, what you're shooting at will not be stationary.

That brings us to the importance of the shot string. Realize that the shot exits the muzzle as an elongated, cigar-shaped cluster. Generally speaking, the tighter the choke the shorter the string, and the more open the choke the longer the string.

Because of this phenomenon, all the pellets don't arrive at the target at the same time. The patterning board tells you where they all ended up—a flat, pancake cluster of pellets—but not the chronology of when they arrived. The stringing of the shot means that some of the pellets you throw at a target may get there before the target reaches the aiming point and some after it leaves that vicinity.

Texan Bob Brister, a national-champion-caliber wingshot and possibly one of the greatest live-bird competition shooters in history, tested the nebulous idea of shot strings in an ingenious manner in his classic book, *Shotgunning, the Art and Science*. Bob strung paper targets on a frame attached to a boat trailer that was towed across a pasture at various speeds while he shot at it. He found that steel shot strings very little because it does not deform (and hence flies truer to the target than malleable lead pellets). The same can be assumed of the newer hard tungsten-based exotics. That's part of the reason why waterfowl gunners had to change their shooting style when forced to forego lead for steel or other non-toxic shots.

The softer (and usually cheaper) the pellets, the longer the string, which means more pellets will be arriving at a specific point over a longer period of time. Cheaper loads increase your margin of error and make it easier to get pellets into the target. That's part of the reason I don't hesitate to use the $2.50-a-box promotional loads on the sporting clays and skeet field (lots of hard crossing targets), while insisting on nitpicking handloads at the trap range where all the birds are climbing and flying away in narrow corridors.

If we were all world-class wingshots shot strings wouldn't be important. However, because the shotgun's main application is to

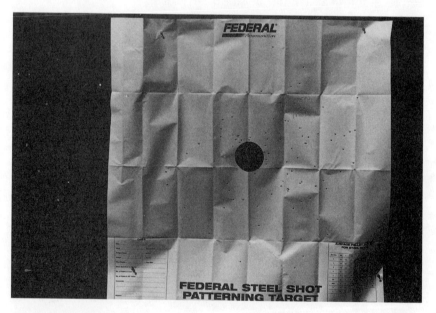

A typical patterning sheet.

shoot at moving targets, the stringing of the shot adds another dimension to the effectiveness. Because of this three-dimensional pattern, which has both an effective width at a given yardage as well as depth into which the target can fly, the shooter has a certain buffer if he or she leads the target too much. The bad news is that if you shoot behind the target, the shot string can't help you score a hit.

Actually, in the old days before plastic wads and/or plating protected the integrity of lead pellets during setback and in their journey down the barrel, shot stringing was an advertising boast among the various ammunition companies.

PATTERNING FOR GUNFIT

Patterning is also useful in gunfitting. In this instance, however, you are not looking at patterning efficiency, but rather where the shot charge centers in relation to a pre-marked aiming point. You can start with a simple test.

The shooter focuses on a marked aiming point, shoulders the gun, and quickly fires. At the Remington Shooting School an instructor would then step in front of the shooter, blocking his or her view of the target, and ask where the shooter thought the pattern would hit. This eliminated making stock adjustments off a shot that may have been accidentally pulled or triggered before the barrel was precisely aimed at the target. Based on a series of patterns fired correctly, an experienced fitter can then determine the proper stock dimensions for that particular shooter.

One technique for verifying fit, or to see if further adjustments are necessary, is to shoot at the pattern board at 16 yards. A trend should emerge from that pattern. Measuring from the center of the aiming point, each inch of displacement translates to a stock adjustment of $\frac{1}{16}$ inch.

If the comb of your gun is too high, you will center your pattern too high. If it's too low, your eye is too low and the pattern will obviously be low, too. A shooter with a pudgy face will generally shoot higher with a particular gun than a thin-faced shooter with the same gun because the mass of the "fuller" face puts the eye in a higher position.

Most American guns are neutral in cast, which means they are not bent toward or away from the shooter's face. But again, the shape of the face will affect the direction of the pattern. If the stock is cast-on, which means there is too much wood on the comb (or that your face is pudgy), your eye will be out of line with the rib or bead and you are likely to shoot off to the left if you are a right-handed shooter (to the right for a lefty). If the stock is cast-off (denoting a thin comb or thin-faced) you are likely to compensate in the other direction.

7

WORKING WITH BEGINNERS

Before we get into the nuts and bolts for starting shotgunners, I must acknowledge the current fact that recommending firearms for kids is not politically correct, which is tragic. It's tragic because the public buys into the seemingly plausible idea that reducing the availability of guns to children will reduce gun violence. But it is obvious that the facts of the matter are just the opposite. Gun accessibility is simply not the problem.

A little common sense proves the point. Consider that gun accessibility in our country has never been as restricted as it is now. I come from an age when members of the school rifle team brought their .22 target rifles to school on the bus. A new shotgun was a very common and eagerly anticipated gift for a boy's 12th or 14th birthday.

My friends and I would hunt on the way to school, store the guns in the trunk of the car in the school parking lot, and hunt again after school. For more than half of my life there were no restrictions on purchasing a long gun or ammunition. Virtually anyone could buy a foreign military rifle through a catalog (for less than what you'd pay for a good steak dinner today) and have it shipped directly to his house.

When confronted with these facts, we must answer the question: With greater youth accessibility to guns in the past, why wasn't there the kind of violence we see with today's much more restricted access to guns?

The answer is respect. It was, in my youth, common to see guns hanging on the wall, leaning behind doors, or in closets, mud rooms, pickups, and bedrooms. They were certainly accessible, but we saw them as untouchable. We knew if we ever wanted to shoot we would have to earn the privilege. That meant obeying the rules of the family and society—showing respect. We used toy guns to act out our adolescent fantasies, but we never crossed the line of pointing a real gun at anybody. We knew the difference and respected it.

We will not make inroads into the gun-violence problem until we acknowledge the underlying causes of youth behavior today compared to yesterday. We must come to the realization that laws

Teaching youngsters respect for firearms is the best solution to gun violence.

and regulations alone cannot produce a civilized society. Morality is society's first line of defense against uncivilized behavior.

Before even handling a gun, the new shooter must learn to respect it and the rules of its use. Okay, enough said. Let's step down from the soapbox and examine some ways to introduce novices painlessly and successfully to shotgunning.

STARTING YOUNG

Way back when, before childhood was redefined by the microchip and cathode-ray tube, it was natural to spend one's adolescence outdoors. Today, if a youngster even finds time to show an early interest in an outdoors endeavor such as hunting or shooting there is a good chance—indeed a distinct probability—that interest will eventually be diluted by myriad other diversions.

Starting off right can lead to a lifetime of shooting.

The common sense approach for a beginning shotgunner includes not spending top dollar on anything that stands a chance of being outgrown in terms of physical stature or attention span. Quality counts more with experience.

If your kids are truly interested in shooting, I'm sure they'd love to start right off shooting your vintage side-by-side. While a certain level of quality in equipment and environment are essential for the novice, there's no need to invest too heavily on what today must be considered a gamble. Regardless of a kid's upbringing or mindset, their reaction to that first head-shot squirrel or wounded doe thrashing in the brush is unpredictable. Some will show excitement while others will be repulsed, and there's no real way of knowing ahead of time.

We owe it to the new shooter—and to the future of shooting and hunting—to make the process as simple, enjoyable, and educational as possible. So start easy, and inexpensively, but make sure you're starting the right way. Remember, you only get one chance to make a first impression.

First of all, depending on the circumstances, you may have to accept the fact that you are not a professional educator and that someone else may be better suited for introducing your son or daughter to the basics of gun handling, safety, and shooting. A shooting program through the local 4-H, Police Athletic League, or local sportsmen's club is a great way to whet young appetites—or at least test young attitudes—for shooting and hunting.

SAFETY

Any shooting program should teach safe gun handling, but it must be reinforced at all times when teaching a newcomer.

Treating the gun as if it were loaded at all times, keeping the safety engaged until the gun is pointed at a target, and being ever-conscious of where the muzzle is pointing are absolutes that can't be overlooked. As a young hunter, I remember spending a couple of days afield toting an empty shotgun after an episode of careless handling. A gun's terrifying potential for destruction can never be ignored.

Carrying the gun so that the muzzle is pointed either skyward or in the direction you are walking is of paramount importance, yet the observant gunner will see this rule broached even by veteran shooters and hunters. How many times have you seen shotguns carelessly slung over shoulders, pointed behind the carrier? It's inexcusable and should be corrected every time, regardless of the person or situation.

When afield, the newcomer should be constantly reminded to be aware of the shooting background; when it's all right to shoot and when to pass up a shot. Small bird shot has a much more limited range than, say, buckshot or slugs, but all can carry farther than you think and should never be fired in a direction where the background is even remotely unsafe. It's a good idea, even with experienced shooters, to remind each other of safety issues before going afield.

For safety and courtesy, a firearm should always be carried with the muzzle facing forward or skyward.

Dove hunters stationed around a sunflower patch or field should remind each other not to shoot at low angles or in the direction of other people, despite the distance between them. Similarly, hunters shooting over dogs should not shoot at low-flying birds, lest a dog leap into harm's way at the flush. Waterfowl hunters in a blind or bird hunters in a field should designate in what direction each will shoot so that barrels don't swing wildly when a bird flies in a particular direction.

The same basic gun control is required of big game hunters also, although they are not often shooting in tandem at animals. Being absolutely, positively sure of your target—and anything in the background—is even more important while big game hunting because the projectile(s) often carries much farther than a pattern of small shot.

Consider also that those with you when the trigger is pulled receive the same—if not more—effect in terms of concussion, flying debris, and noise. Always know where your hunting companions are when you shoot.

Ear and eye protection is a must in any shooting endeavor, both for safety and to avoid an unpleasant experience for a novice shooter or youngster.

INTRODUCTION TO SHOOTING

A single-shot .22 rifle is an excellent learning tool for youngsters and a staple of most organized introductory programs. Its workings and operation are obvious and simple. It fits young bodies, demands trigger control for accuracy, and doesn't dole out punishment.

After acquainting a youngster with the safe handling and operating of firearms through the .22, it's a logical but large step into shotguns. In introducing a novice to shotgunning, make sure that the shotgun fits the shooter. Generally speaking, novices will be youngsters or women, and hence smaller-framed than the average adult male for whom most firearms are designed. A small-framed person needs a smaller gun; one that is as user-friendly as possible. Recoil is generally heavy in shotguns and shooting one that doesn't fit the shooter will result in much more heavily felt recoil.

Virtually every shotgun manufacturer makes a short-stock, thin-grip "youth" or even "ladies" model, usually in 20-gauge, with a trigger pull around 12½ inches compared to the standard 14. Winchester, Remington, Browning, Ithaca, Savage, Marlin, Mossberg, and other gunmakers all offer youth/ladies models that are smaller-stocked versions of their flagship shotgun designs. The barrels and actions come off the same machines as the higher-priced, fancier-finished models in the same lines. The major difference is usually the shorter stock and a metal finish.

If that first firearm sparks the novice's interest for more, you can always upgrade a youth-model gun by simply replacing the

Use a little common sense when introducing a youngster to shotgunning. Recoil sours attitudes quickly.

stock with an adult version or by moving up to another gun if the infatuation with shooting turns out to be more than a passing phase.

It is the ultimate folly to start a novice off with a heavy, big-bore gun and "let them grow into it." When teaching someone to drive, you don't put the driver's seat back too far for them to reach the pedals and steering wheel in the hope that they will "grow into it." It's just as important that they have a usable system for learning to shoot.

While smaller people simply need smaller shotguns, beware of that fact as well. If a gun has a lot of drop in the comb of the stock, the sensation of recoil will be even greater. Fitting squarely into that category are "youth" 20-gauge, single-shot guns regrettably chambered for 3-inch loads. They may feel light to carry, but that joy makes an immediate about-face when the trigger is pulled. Smaller shooters do, however, need something with less weight that can be supported by smaller arms; something with a shorter stock that keeps the center of gravity to the rear and affords a comfortable reach to the trigger.

The grip and forearm size is as important as stock length when fitting a smaller-statured shooter. A large grip in small hands doesn't allow sufficient thumb-over placement, stretches the hand to reach the trigger, and accentuates felt recoil.

The problem we face is that smaller shotguns kick harder, and recoil is something we're trying to control if not avoid. It is the single most intimidating factor in shooting. Manliness, unfortunately, is seemingly measured in foot-pounds. But I maintain that we shouldn't be reading testosterone on the chronograph. We should clear that up for novice shooters right away. Given the effectiveness of today's loads, the 20-gauge is no longer a popgun. It is a logical starting gun, given its reduced recoil and lack of heft.

Pump shotguns kick less than breechloaders only because they are marginally heavier. The added weight slows the recoil reaction since the explosion simply has more mass to move. But while the pump is probably almost universally seen as the optimum starting gun, I see that as a common mistake. People like them because they are inexpensive, simple, and durable. They are also relatively light to carry, but that lack of heft translates to big recoil.

My choice for breaking in new shooters is an autoloader. Load one shell at a time if you want to limit the new shooter's firepower, yet take advantage of that action's recoil- or gas-operated system to greatly reduce recoil.

Yes, autoloaders cost more and weigh more. But if you can get past the first point, you can get around the second one. The Remington 1100 Youth Model, which comes in 20-gauge, is as light as most pumpguns, yet it has the recoil-absorbing quality of the autoloader.

Regardless of your choice of action, recoil can be tamed further in a couple of ways. An aftermarket recoil pad will likely be thicker and more efficient than the one that came with the gun. Recoil can also be reduced by installing mercury suppression cylinders, sometimes called "Dead Mules," in the buttstock or magazine of the gun. These simple but extremely effective items work on basic physics: a counterweight blunts the rearward rush of the gun during recoil and spreads out the effect over a longer period of time. It's the same basic principle that is behind the gas cylinder in gas-operated autoloaders.

Porting the barrel—having a gunsmith drill holes in the top of the barrel near the muzzle to vent the gases before the load leaves the muzzle—also serves to limit barrel jump and felt recoil.

Stock fit and its relation to felt recoil have already been mentioned. But no matter how well a stock conforms to the shooter, if the comb is too low to allow comfortable cheek placement—and many shotgun combs are—a comb lift can be added economically. Leather, lace-on Monte Carlo pads are available through Cabela's, as are foam pads from Beartooth that simply slide on, or others that adhere to the stock.

As to loads, the reduced payload of the 20-gauge load, of course, means less recoil than a 12-gauge, but proper choice in ammunition is another factor. Use light target loads when hunting birds and small game, or low-recoil slugs when deer hunting with youngsters. The lack of firepower will likely be offset by the fact that the shooter will be less intimidated.

My daughter started out with the short-stocked Remington 1100 Youth 20-gauge and grew into the longer-stocked version that sometimes accompanies Dad to the sporting clays range. The gun has provided a lot of pleasant shooting experiences. She didn't take a beating and neither did Dad's wallet.

Above all, we want the novice and small-statured shooter to have a positive experience. That means making the shotgun as comfortable and user-friendly as possible.

SHOOTING GUIDELINES

I've worked with various hunting education programs and teachers for years. Based on that experience, here are some guidelines I've come up with to help maintain interest and hopefully build a future shooting and hunting partner:

- Keep sessions and equipment simple. Make it fun, not intimidating or confusing.
- Don't shoot or hunt too seriously in the presence of kids. Nothing turns a teen off faster than a parent's negative actions.
- In the beginning, keep the sessions short. When the action is slow, or sometimes even when it's hot, kids have a short attention span. It's always best to leave a kid wanting more.
- Start out shooting at easy targets and hunting plentiful game. Kids want results.

- If a shooting or hunting session lags or gets tedious, be prepared to put the guns up and do something else for awhile. Take a nature walk with or without the guns; make a contest out of tree or bird identification; read the sights, sounds, and wind—make it a memorable experience even if you fall short of the original goals.
- If you're hunting, make sure to bring a change of clothes for your young partner and have something fun to eat—lots of it.
- Observe very strict safety rules. Regardless of the fun, this is a learning experience.
- But remember that this is supposed to be fun. Don't let lagging interest or childish attitudes discourage you. The whole idea is to foster a lifelong interest.

HEARING PROTECTION

Hearing and eye protection are standards at organized shooting events today and are staples on the shooting range. But it hasn't always been so. In fact, in my youth I don't remember anyone wearing protection while shooting.

The first time I realized there was a problem was when it was documented at my military pre-induction physical. Like I said, nobody wore hearing protection back then. Sure, the old ears buzzed after shooting, but I always felt that was part of the deal. After all, when the buzzing stopped the hearing came back; didn't it? Well, I'm here to tell you now that thinking your damaged hearing will come back makes about as much sense as leaving the porch light on for Jimmy Hoffa. It's gone and it's going to stay gone.

Over the years I've lost more than 50 percent of the hearing ability in my left ear and slightly less than that in the right (a typical scenario for a right-handed shooter, whose right ear is partially closed—and thus protected—by that cheek's contact with the

Hearing and eye protection is a must whenever you operate a firearm.

stock). I find myself reading lips during conversations at parties or when the television or radio is playing—anywhere there is background noise.

Now I wear hearing protection whenever I'm at the range. Constantly. It's part of the outfit now, to save what little hearing I have left. To be honest, it feels a little like closing the barn door after the horse has escaped.

The effects of muzzle blast on hearing are well documented. Hearing loss from exposure to repeated gunfire is gradual, incremental, and irreversible. The consensus among hearing experts is that prolonged exposure to sound levels around 130 decibels can eventually result in damaged hearing.

Not many of us have the foggiest notion how loud 130 decibels is. For reference, rifles tested at the U.S. Army Proving Grounds in Aberdeen, Maryland produced sound-pressure levels at 160 to 172.5

Walker's Game Ear makes hearing enhancement and protection devices that are popular with hunters and shooters.

decibels—which ain't healthy. Short-barreled firearms produced exceptionally sharp reports; the muzzle blast is simply closer to your ears. You may be surprised to learn that a 12-gauge shotgun blast produces about 140 decibels. Pistols are even louder.

"You've got to remember that you're not only ravaging your ears every time you shoot, but every time someone shoots around you," says audiologist and hunter Bob Walker of Media, Pennsylvania. Walker came onto the outdoor scene several years ago with the introduction of his Game Ear, a device with the same circuitry as a $600–$700 hearing aid that was designed to heighten a hunter's awareness while in the woods yet shut off noises like gunfire.

Earmuffs are the most efficient protection devices available, resulting in a reduction of 30 to 45 decibels. The hardcover muffs reflect sound off their outer shells and also muffle sound inside through dead air space. Several companies make excellent models with amplifiers built in so that the wearer isn't cut off from natural, unobtrusive sounds.

There are plenty of plug-type inserts, from custom molded silicone rubber devices to sponge rubber plugs. Most, when properly inserted, provide adequate protection. A little cotton or paper (remember using cigarette butts?) stuffed in an ear, however, provides minimal protection.

Hearing protection is not only a safety precaution, it also helps some shooters improve their scores. By significantly dampening noise, ear protectors help shooters concentrate better.

Take it from a guy who learned the hard way. Leave the macho image behind when you go to the range or field. Wear hearing protection and save your future.

8

THE ART OF WINGSHOOTING

For my money, successful wingshooting is the most difficult concept to master of any sport. Period. Sure, hitting a baseball with a bat is often described as the most difficult; and most of us find that consistently hitting a golf ball straight and long is a nearly impossible task. But if you rank either of these efforts as tougher than wingshooting, you've probably never seriously tried shooting a firearm offhand at a flying target. Having played baseball at the semiprofessional level and being competitive on the golf course today, I'm here to tell you that a good sporting clays course makes a batter's box or fairway look like a toddler's sandbox in comparison.

Granted, all three exercises are intimidating and difficult. All require a modicum of eye-to-hand coordination and physical flexibility. But wingshooting is more difficult simply because of the space, logistics, and equipment needed to participate and the lack of interested or qualified instructors. After all, a kid can learn to hit with a little instruction and a batting tee, and a golf pro can teach you a repeatable golf swing in a couple of lessons, but becoming an effective wingshot takes an expert watching over the student's shoulder on a range where clay birds can be thrown with repetitive accuracy—a combination that isn't easy for the novice shooter to find (or afford).

Entire books have been written just about the mechanics of wingshooting, and there are many videos on the subject. While these are helpful, it is still a difficult sport to learn without expert, on-the-spot instruction in the fundamentals, followed by lots of practice.

Making sure your gun fits you properly—as discussed earlier in this book—is the first step in good shooting. When the stock touches your cheek, the gun should be lined up to shoot where your eyes are focused. (Testing your shotgun on the patterning board should have given you a good feel for this.)

Let's take a look at the types of wingshooting methods and the basic elements of good form.

Master the mechanics of wing-shooting and you'll have many fulfilling days in the field.

SHOOTING METHODS

Wingshooting instructors shoot with varying proficiency and teach varying styles. Some teach mechanical methods of sustained-lead, pull-through, or even spot shooting. Others teach the Churchill method or variations of the purely instinctive style.

Sustained-lead shooting entails swinging the muzzle a given distance in front of the target and maintaining that distance while shooting until the follow-through is complete. In practice, sustained lead is easy to learn yet difficult to apply to a variety of shooting conditions. It is, nevertheless, an excellent method for skeet shooting, where all targets are predictable in speed and angle, day-to-day and field-to-field.

Swing-through, or pull-through, is a method in which the muzzle is swung from behind the target, traces the flight path of the target, then the load is triggered as the muzzle swings past or ahead of the target. The move must be continued with a follow-through to

Wingshooting instructor Steve Schultz believes in letting your mind track the target.

assure sufficient muzzle speed. This method is more difficult to learn than sustained lead and requires more practice to keep the timing sharp. But it is more versatile and can be applied to virtually all forms of shotgun shooting.

Most good shooters today practice both methods, along with a manner of instinctive shooting, and employ whatever method works best for the type of target they are confronted with. Although shooting schools follow different formats and teach different methods, the message is basically the same and the results are comparable. Orvis maintains schools on a national basis, as does Remington Arms and Safari Club International, among others. (See the Appendix for a full listing of shooting schools.)

Most schools are generally not a sporting clays teaching academy, although they are often conducted on clays layouts. Instruction is in wingshooting per se, with skeet and trap shooting instruction included where the layout permits. Other schools, like Steve Schultz's SCI Road Show can be customized to fit any club's layout and any student's interests or budget. Less formal instruction is also becoming more prevalent at clays courses nationwide.

THE DOMINANT EYE

Because shotgunners will be shooting with both eyes open and focused on the target, virtually all instructors will start by having students determine their dominant, or "master," eye. If the shooter is cross-dominant—a right-handed person with a dominant left eye or vice-versa, he or she will essentially be looking in a different direction than the gun muzzle is pointed. Not good. To combat this, a spot or even a slight smudge can be placed in a strategic spot on the lens of the shooting glasses over the dominant eye. The spot draws that eye's attention, making the brain rely on the other eye to track the target. Contrary to popular belief, the dominant eye is not stronger, just the one that focuses first.

Determining your dominant, or master, eye is the first step in wingshooting instruction.

There is a simple exercise used to determine one's dominant eye. Look at a distant object, then frame it in a "window" formed by your hands, held palms-out at arm's length. Now close one eye. If the object is still visible, the open eye is dominant. If it disappears, you've closed the dominant eye. One variation of this method is to keep both eyes open and slowly draw your intertwined hands back toward your face. The framing hands will automatically go to the dominant eye.

Once the dominant eye has been determined, the second step is to learn how to stand while swinging and shooting at a moving target.

Shooting with a mounted gun, which is common in skeet, trap, and recreational forms of sporting clays, demands more of the dominant eye—as does the sustained lead or pull-through techniques of shooting. It is less important in instinctive shooting.

THE STANCE

The stance is the foundation of good shooting, just as it is in golf or in hitting. Stand with feet placed almost shoulder-width apart. Weight should be evenly distributed and knees flexed. The basic stance for most targets calls for a right-handed shooter to point his or her left toe (right toe for left-handed shooters) toward the point where they intend to break the bird (assuming you're learning to shoot at a clays course). At address (the ready-to-mount position), the gun barrel should be held halfway between where the bird is first visible and the breaking point. This stance will give the shooter the most efficient body position to swing with the flight of the bird.

Again, knees should always be flexed, a factor that is even more critical on dropping targets. As the gun is mounted, weight should be shifted smoothly to the lead foot so that 70 percent of the weight is

Proper stance plays an important role in consistent shooting.

forward when the trigger is tripped. When done correctly, the left toe and belly button should be facing the bird when the shooter fires.

With sufficient practice the shooter will find himself automatically adjusting his stance to address a target in the field, be it a moving deer or turkey or a flushing bird.

Although it can't be done in all instances, ideally the gun is fired just as it reaches the shooter's cheek in the practiced position. The Remington Shooting School teaches the R.E.M Method: "R" for read the target, "E" for eye contact, and "M" for movement. It is really just a variation of Move, Mount, and Shoot, but that wouldn't fit the sponsoring company's name as well; would it?

LEARNING THE MOVE

A smooth, efficient, practiced move is critical to shooting success, and it starts with pointing the muzzle. One of the basics of professional instructor Steve Schultz's instruction is the pistol shooting

Pointing the index finger of your lead hand at the target will help you stay on track.

The front hand should do most of the work in making a smooth transition from the low-gun position to a fully mounted position.

technique—tracking the target with the index finger of your lead hand, not your trigger finger.

He preaches placing the left index finger along the forend instead of under it, pointing at the target. Holding the gun in this manner allows the shooter the familiar feeling that he's pointing at the target, but it also uses the palm and arm (with a locked wrist) as a lever to move the barrel in a much more efficient method than the common palm-under hold.

Allowing the lead hand to control the movement start to finish—sort of like a golf swing—is the one absolutely essential element in successful wingshooting. Let the trigger hand take charge at any point, even for a fraction of a second, and the muzzle will move off line.

From a low-gun position, start your move to mount the gun with the lead hand, pointing that index finger toward the target. Let the trigger hand follow but not guide. You do use the trigger hand to guide the stock up to the ledge of your cheekbone while keeping your head still. Put the stock comb in that spot on your cheek consistently, and the butt will automatically slide into position on your shoulder.

It all has to be one smooth move. Economy of motion. Do what is needed and nothing more. One motion, deliberate yet fluid.

The typical shooter doesn't do that. He brings the gunbutt up and back to his shoulder with his trigger hand, drops his head to the stock, then goes looking for the target—which he'll undoubtedly have to chase. When the trigger hand takes charge the muzzle moves off track. And moving the head short-circuits the essential eye-hand coordination. Put gunbutt to shoulder first and the muzzle won't stay on the target path; the lead hand must lead from start to finish.

Schultz advises students to practice the mount in front of a mirror, focusing their eyes on the muzzle reflection. Once the correct mount is achieved, it should be repeated on a daily basis to make it an instinctive rather than mechanical move. A second exercise is to mount the gun and trace the line of your ceiling in each direction over and over. These two exercises repeated in a focused manner for just three or four minutes a day for a couple of weeks will train you surprisingly well.

THE INSTINCTIVE SHOOTER

Instinctive shooting is the most commonly taught method, although virtually all instructors (American instructors, anyway) also teach the sustained lead and pull-through methods to cover all situations. I've found that Schultz's droll, witty, down-home style and keen insights turn the fairly complex activity of hitting flying targets with a shotgun blast into an achievable talent. So let's follow him through some additional training steps for new shooters.

His simple method teaches coordination between eyes and hands through simple exercises and repetition. Once achieved, that

Professional instructors are a huge help in mastering the basics of wingshooting.

can serve as a foundation for the mastering of specific shooting styles both on clay target ranges and in bird hunting.

"We teach you how to use the most powerful computer circuitry in the world, the one between your ears," said Schultz, former director of the Houston-based American Shooting Center. For instance, one of the most commonly asked questions in duck blinds or on clays courses is "How much lead are you giving the bird?" But Schultz doesn't use the word "lead."

"How can you teach it?" Steve says. "Sustained lead requires so much computation, it's almost all experience—there is no consistent way to judge distance against open sky, speed, and so on. You can compute that a target flying 40 mph at a right angle to you 40 yards away requires 14 feet of lead, but what if it's actually 35 or 45 yards and coming at an angle of 60 degrees rather than 90? Let your brain do the mathematics. It has the capacity if you'll eliminate the obstacles. It's the same instinctive calculation that you use when throwing a ball or making a basketball shot."

Steve says that instead of determining lead and chasing the target with a mechanical motion, you should tailor your gun position so that it's pointing right where you are looking. Then simply look at the nose of the target while maintaining the swing.

"If the end of the barrel is doing what the bird is doing, you'll never miss," he says.

The idea is to keep from aiming—sighting down the barrel—at the target. Steve maintains that gunmakers put beads (he calls them "miss me" beads) on shotguns just to sell you more shells. The bead draws your eye to the barrel, which invariably stops its movement and causes a miss.

A bird in the hand is the ultimate reward for practicing your shooting.

"You can't see the target when you're looking at the tool," Steve notes. "Ever try to watch the hammer while you're trying to drive a nail? Do you watch the bat when you're trying to hit a baseball, or the club during your golf swing?

"Once you've eliminated extra thoughts, you can focus on the shot and let your training take over. Thinking too much, cluttering the brain with ideas when you actually want it to react instinctively, is a major reason for missing. Don't think. It gets in the way. Send me the dumb blonde they tell jokes about and I'll have her Olympic caliber in six weeks."

Putting all the elements of good stance and technique together in one smooth motion and letting your eyes and the barrel find the target without conscious thought takes time—and a lot of practice—to master, but it's the basis for all good wingshooting.

9

WATERFOWL HUNTING

My wingshooting instincts kicked in just as the long-circling flock of geese committed. Wings set, feet down, a dozen big Canadas began their final descent into the decoys. But suddenly the lead bird saw something it didn't like. With a panicked staccato cackle, the goose suddenly reversed engines, pumping its wings madly in a desperate attempt to regain altitude. The others, exhibiting the extraordinary telepathy that flocking birds seem to possess, immediately followed his lead.

"Take 'em!" shouted my hunting partner, Chuck.

I sat up from my cornstalk-covered hide, the gun simultaneously gliding to the familiar stockweld on my cheek as I slid the muzzle just past the beak of one of the nearest birds and touched off the shot. The goose was a little more than 40 yards away, but the lead apparently wasn't enough. Okay, maybe I pulled the shot. At any rate, the pattern centered the 9-pound bird's body rather than its head and neck. Ripped and dislodged feathers flew in a corona around the desperate bird—yet its wings kept pumping. The tattered feathers were still floating to the ground when the bird, its wings set, glided out of sight over the horizon of cornstalks.

"That's that new stuff, ain't it?" my partner said with barely disguised disgust as he kicked off the cornstalks in preparation to march out and retrieve the bird that he'd downed. "Just like steel used to be. That bird's dead but don't know it yet. Now we'll have to use up hunting time to look for him or he'll be coyote bait."

The waterfowling world quickly came up with steel as an alternative to lead shot when the feds started mandating a change in the 1980s. But much of the last decade of the twentieth century was spent looking for an acceptable alternative to steel. The U.S. Fish & Wildlife Service has since approved steel, bismuth-tin, tungsten-iron, tungsten-polymer, tungsten-iron-steel, and tungsten-nickel (Hevi-Shot) shot.

The latest generation of steel alternatives, the newest tungsten-derivative loads, show great promise while the others have their disadvantages. But the price and, in some instances, performance factors of some alternatives may make steel look like a wise choice.

Nontoxic shot may have cleaned up waterways, but it also cleaned out the wallets of most waterfowlers.

Steel shot was originally opposed by hunters because its extreme hardness imperiled the barrels of old shotguns. It lost its energy much quicker than lead due to its reduced density, and steel's internal ballistics required a slower, far dirtier burning powder. It was also prone to rusting in its hull; and its patterns were too tight and shot string too short, which required a different sight picture and lead on flying birds.

And, of course, it cost considerably more than lead shot.

But in the 1960s "lead" became a four-letter word in a world of expanding environmental awareness, and steel became a necessity for waterfowlers. Although it's long been a munitions designer's dream metal, lead's poisonous qualities began manifesting themselves in the outdoors. A landmark biological study by USFWS research biologist Frank Bellrose in 1957 determined that a considerable percentage of ducks were dying of lead poisoning after ingesting spent pellets from the bottoms of ponds and lakes. Raptors were in turn imperiled when they fed on the carcasses of the poisoned ducks. Consequently, waterfowl hunting was led down the politically-correct road.

Despite hunters, the National Rifle Association, and myriad other organizations questioning the veracity of the study and the effectiveness of shot made of anything but lead, the feds stood their ground. More than 20 years ago non-toxic shot became mandated in critical areas of various flyways and was gradually phased in as the only legal load for waterfowl until the entire country was covered in 1991. Canada followed in 1996.

Now the Environmental Protection Agency has picked up the banner and has made proposals to take lead out of fishing and, eventually, target shooting and upland game hunting. The non-toxic wave is upon us, and waterfowlers are the test pilots for the rest of the shooting and hunting industry.

Initial steel loads were indeed pathetic and ineffective. But years of research and development followed at Winchester-Olin,

Autoloaders like the Browning Gold (left) and Winchester Super-X2 help reduce the recoil from large goose loads.

Federal Cartridge, and Remington, resulting in vastly improved steel loads and performance. Most shooters adjusted, and some accepted the inevitable. Waterfowlers were convinced that steel was inferior, but if they wanted to hunt it was their only choice. The anguished cries lessened but were never really silenced.

To be honest, today's waxed, copper-plated steel or zinc-galvanized (to prevent rusting and choke damage) buffered loads are very effective on geese out to 40 yards in most shot sizes. High-velocity loads from Federal and Winchester push that envelope even further. Winchester's revolutionary new manufacturing process is also making steel loads more affordable.

SELECTING CHOKES

In the early years of steel shot's use for waterfowl hunting, the rule of thumb was to open chokes at least one constriction more for steel than you did for lead. Steel pellets were much harder, therefore less susceptible to deformation than lead, and thus threw a tighter pattern without as much constriction. But as technology advanced in steel-shot loadings and choke tubes, that thinking has changed a bit. It's not so simple anymore.

Shooters are finding that a modified choke no longer throws steel loads in patterns that fit within full-choke parameters like they once did. At least not in the smaller sizes, such as No. 2s through 6s or 8s. Today's smaller pellets spread well with open chokes, but through modified chokes they pretty much shoot patterns that fit within conventional parameters.

Large steel shot, however—and I'm talking No. 1s and BBs and even F shot—quite often will throw a full-choke pattern through a modified choke. Of course, it will vary with chamber size, barrel, and the brand of choke you use, but generally speaking, steel shot patterning is changing.

Tungsten-iron patterned much like steel (much denser patterns), but subsequent exotics such as bismuth-tin, tungsten-polymer, tungsten-matrix, and Hevi-Shot exhibited patterning characteristics much like lead loads. The harder shot also required a different shooting technique since the shot string was much shorter. Lead shot strings were as long as 12 feet when the pattern passed 40 yards, requiring a much longer lead than steel shot or tungsten.

While virtually all shotgun manufacturers have a waterfowl or "steel shot" choke tube, there are also a host of aftermarket tubes available. Because the relationship between the diameter of the choke tube and the interior diameter of the barrel determines the actual constriction, a specific choke tube will pattern differently in a variety of guns. In fact, some aftermarket choke companies (Angleport by Ballistic Specialties, Rhino, Seminole Gun Works, Briley, and so on) prefer to fit the tube to the exact dimension of your personal barrel for optimum performance.

BISMUTH, THE FIRST NON-STEEL NON-TOXIC

In the early 1990s bismuth became a front-runner among the lead-replacement wannabes. Before that a Canadian ballistician was designing bismuth alloy mixes and loads and eventually enlisted a couple of British companies to load them. With U.S. waterfowlers frowning at steel, American developers became interested and the Bismuth Cartridge Company of Dallas, Texas was formed. It, too, enlisted the British to assemble the early loadings.

Bismuth Cartridge was a very small firm, lacking the squads of lawyers and researchers needed to influence the U.S. Fish & Wildlife Service. Thus, bismuth's acceptance by USFWS was delayed until 1995.

When Federal Cartridge Company introduced its Premium tungsten-iron loads in 1996, munitions giant Winchester-Olin

Goose hunters now have more loads to choose from than ever before.

quickly formed an alliance with Bismuth Cartridge to offset its competitor's potential advantage in the waterfowl market. The partnership was dissolved in 2000.

So what is bismuth? Well, the scholarly will note that it is an inert elemental metal that sits squarely between lead (Pb) and polonium (Po) in the Periodic Table of Elements. It has a specific gravity very close to that of lead (91 percent) and is about 14 percent lighter. Like steel, it's damned hard but malleable enough (when mixed with 3 or 4 percent tin) to be molded into round pellets. (Trivia buffs will note that bismuth is the chief ingredient in the timeless upset stomach remedy Pepto-Bismol.)

Several years ago, while patterning some early-generation bismuth loads, I found that the pellets actually shattered upon setback on occasion. In later field-testing, I saw very little indication of shattering in the then newly buffered Bismuth Cartridge loadings. But when shooting through skinned chicken carcasses, some of the bismuth pellets left very small slivers in the flesh.

Regardless of its popularity, bismuth has not and will not flood the market. There simply isn't very much of the stuff available in the few American and South American mines unearthing it. But it's a start.

"Bismuth is good, but it's not the ultimate answer," said one industry insider just before Winchester stepped out of the marketing agreement. "From a profit standpoint there's too many entities involved."

It should be noted that Winchester then negotiated with EnviroMetal for the exclusive right to market Hevi-Shot but balked at the numbers, which is when Remington stepped in.

TUNGSTEN-BASED LOADS

The next big breakthrough after bismuth was Federal's tungsten-iron load, which might be more accurately named "improved steel." Given tungsten's extreme hardness, copious amounts of iron must be added in order to soften the alloy sufficiently to die-form and heat-sinter it into pellets. Federal's Premium Tungsten pellets are actually 60 percent iron and 40 percent tungsten. (Tungsten-iron was the load used during the goose hunting trip described at the beginning of this chapter.)

"Pellet softness, the ability to deform on impact, is more important from a lethality standpoint than density," said one noted shotshell ballistician.

No sooner had complaints about its extreme hardness begun to ring out than Federal introduced a softer, better performing tungsten-polymer load. Kent Cartridge, a Canadian firm that in 1998 took over the facilities at the financially plagued Activ complex in West Virginia, followed Federal's lead with a virtually identical (in a performance sense) tungsten-matrix load (which uses tin in the alloy).

"There's not a thing wrong with tungsten-polymer or matrix," noted the same ballistician, who will remain anonymous due to the fact that his company doesn't manufacture those products. "It's resilient. It deforms well on impact. It drags feathers into the wound channel. It just kills real well."

In fact, the tungsten-polymer or matrix loads virtually mirror lead loads in ballistics, performance, and efficiency. The drawback is that in softening the alloy, patterning becomes inconsistent. That's the reasoning behind the development of Federal's duplex tungsten-iron-steel load, which consists of a layer of steel pellets laid over a layer of tungsten-iron pellets.

The theory behind duplex loads is that they will pattern extremely well, with the steel helping to fill in pattern density at short ranges and the tungsten-iron carrying its energy much farther downrange. In my experience, however, while duplex loads look good on a patterning board, reducing the advantages of both pellets by cutting their respective numbers just waters down overall performance.

Marketing of the tungsten-iron load touts the fact that it is 94 percent as dense as lead, 32 percent denser than steel, and 10 percent denser than bismuth. It is also 30 percent harder than steel, which should throw up a red flag for seasoned observers. I've seen tungsten-iron BBs blow right through 20-gauge galvanized sheet metal at 30 yards—handy if you have to defend yourself against small aircraft but too much zip without deformation to be regularly effective on waterfowl.

Like steel, due to its hardness, tungsten-iron shot should not be fired through double guns or older thin-walled barrels or choke tube systems—areas where bismuth and lead are acceptable. Tungsten-iron patterns tighter than bismuth or lead, much like steel loads, since the hardness of the pellets limits deformity at setback or through chokes. The tungsten-iron pellets are so hard that a very thick plastic wad must be employed to protect barrel walls. The wad takes up more room in the hull than do wads in the other loads, leaving less space for pellets.

Despite the marketing blitz that is putting Federal Premium tungsten-iron at the forefront of high-tech legal goose loads, I've always felt that its performance as a hunting load was significantly inferior to that of Winchester-Bismuth or the other Federal or Kent tungsten loads, despite the higher price tag. Tungsten-iron's potential is also limited by the difficulty of manufacture, due largely to tungsten's hardness. Smaller pellet loads will simply be difficult to develop.

New tungsten-polymers and matrix and bismuths demonstrated superiority in energy transfer and wound channel size, which makes them better killing loads than tungsten-iron. Bismuth approaches lead load performance and the polymer and matrix loads match it, while tungsten-iron comes off as a simple improvement over steel.

Meanwhile, tungsten-polymer and matrix pellets pattern almost like lead, which is what we're all looking for in a non-toxic alternative. And, like bismuth-tin, they can be shot through any gun.

Success in a goose blind has a lot to do with your choice of load.

They throw a far more forgiving spread than steel or tungsten-iron and exhibit shot-stringing characteristics nearly identical to those of high-brass lead loads.

Both bench and field tests showed that the Federal tungsten-polymer and Kent tungsten-matrix loads were marginal improvements over bismuth. The tungsten offshoots were virtually identical to each other in ballistics and performance.

Overall, it will take an awfully sensitive hand with a shotgun to notice the performance difference between lead and bismuth-tin or the newer tungsten polymer and matrix loads.

THE CASE FOR HEVI-SHOT

As noted, steel shot has improved remarkably since its introduction. But the fact remains that there is still a huge drop-off in performance when compared to lead.

"The industry has been looking for an alternative to steel since the first day it was introduced," says former Winchester-Olin Technical Marketing Services chief Mike Jordan, the company's leading load designer in those days. "There were lots of substances to choose from, but each one seemed to have its drawbacks either in performance or accessibility or it wasn't acceptable to the environmental community. That, and they all cost a lot more. The alternatives that have been accepted have their drawbacks. They are not the final answer; we're still looking."

An industry that has looked at everything from depleted uranium to molybeum and varied polymers to polysyllabic entities only a metallurgist could love is still seeking the ultimate non-toxic shot. If early testing is any indication, Hevi-Shot may be the answer—at least for now.

When I first handled Hevi-Shot I nearly dismissed it as another over-hyped, overpriced, non-toxic shotshell. The first hull I opened looked like junk; the pellets were spherical and irregularly shaped rather than round. How would that ever pattern efficiently?

The answer is in the density of the remarkable tungsten-nickel alloy. Mass is the overriding factor in good shotshell patterns. Jay Menefee of Polywad Company, who loaded Hevi-Shot for the EnvironMetal Company before Remington picked up the banner in 2001, compares it to the phenomenon of a misshapen rock flying straighter than a perfectly round Ping-Pong ball. Hevi-Shot was an immediately visible improvement in patterning, and that's what we're looking for in the goose field.

Hevi-Shot is a totally different tungsten-nickel-iron combination than those tungsten exotics produced by Federal Cartridge and Kent Cartridge recently and is less expensive per box. The pellets are heavier (relative to their size) than any civilian-available shotshell pellets and thus can carry farther and hit harder. (This is due to the reduced air resistance to small, heavy pellets that can maintain energy comparable to much larger pellets of lighter material.) They are heavier than lead (specific density of 11.8 vs. 11.2 for pure lead), and they're heavier still than lead pellets containing lightweight antimony.

The only drawback that I can see in Hevi-Shot is that—like steel and tungsten-iron—it can't be shot through double barrels or old shotgun barrels or chokes due to its hardness.

The retail prices for all these alternatives, however, may well make waterfowlers find they don't hate steel as much as they thought they did. Federal Premium, Winchester Supreme, and Remington Nitro 3-inch 12-gauge steel loads will cost you about 55 to 60 cents a shot (70 cents for 3½-inchers). Comparable 3-inch tungsten-iron loads from Federal will be $2 a shot and Federal tungsten-polymer and tungsten-matrix from Kent $1.90 every time you pull the trigger. None of those loads come in 3½-inch hulls yet. Meanwhile, 3-inch Winchester bismuth loads will cost about $1.80 per shot and $2.40 per shot if you use the 3½-inch version. Hevi-Shot costs in excess of $2 a shot.

The advent of steel shot and its attendant lack of energy compared to lead made 3-inch loads a minimum for waterfowling, and despite the harder-hitting bismuth and tungsten alloys, you will have difficulty finding a waterfowl load shorter than three inches.

What's the best? If you are pass-shooting ducks on a river or over decoys where the shooting is generally less than 35 yards, No. 2 or 4 steel is just fine. Bismuth and tungsten can certainly be used, but they are far more expensive and simply not necessary at that range. If you are into big-field goose hunting or big-water duck hunting, the non-toxic exotics, with their better retained energy, are more in line. You can go with big-pellet steel (as large as BB, T, or even F) or smaller pellets in bismuth or tungsten alloys.

In my book, the 3½-inch 12-gauge is overkill, but the fact remains that you get marginally more pellets in the pattern. From the shooter's perspective, 3-inch guns are plenty during a heavy day of shooting, and the 3-inch versions of tungsten-alloy loads—particularly Hevi-Shot—will kill at longer ranges than most hunters can accurately shoot anyway.

I shoot 3-inch steel over close-range decoys and when pass-shooting, and Hevi-Shot for geese in fields. I find that the latter is easier to pattern than other tungsten mixes. If I can't find Hevi-Shot (which sometimes happens if the season's allotment is depleted early), bismuth, tungsten-matrix, or tungsten-polymer are very suitable alternatives. Bismuth is also safe with older guns that might not be suitable for steel or tungsten because of softer barrel steel.

10

SHOTGUNNING FOR BIG GAME

I'd been watching a steep grassy hillside below the browned CRP field, seeing six bucks and as many does from my treestand perch in the first two days. The final morning was no different, with two small-racked bucks chasing does, and each other, across the hillside. Any rack normally will do for me, but this was Illinois's frenetic 3-day early shotgun season in the "Golden Triangle" defined by the junction of the Illinois and Missouri Rivers. For my money, it's the best opportunity for a truly big buck in the lower 48 states, and I was being uncharacteristically choosy.

At about 10:00 A.M. something sailed out of the tall CRP grass and caught my eye. I didn't know what it was until the buck landed on the hillside and sprinted downhill toward the wooded creek bottom to my left.

At first glance he looked like a shooter, but I had only a split second to evaluate his rack, get the gun up, and take aim before he bolted into the trees at the bottom of the hill. At about 100 yards it would have been a slam-dunk shot for a rifleman, but Illinois doesn't allow centerfires. So quick-judging the distance, I got the sprinting buck in the slug gun's scope, swung the crosshairs ahead of his chest, and tripped the 2.5-pound trigger.

In a feeling borne of experience, I was confident of the sight picture and familiar trigger pull and was rewarded with a loud crashing sound in the trees where he'd disappeared.

I found the big 9-pointer suspended in two splintered saplings where he'd died in mid-stride just 25 yards from where the slug hit him. At a distance I would later laser-rangefind at 118 yards, the 1,800-feet-per-second Lightfield Commander slug had caught the buck at the tip of the left shoulder and angled back and down through both lungs, tearing away the aorta at the top of his heart before smashing a rib and exiting the far side. Perfect performance.

Again, it was an easy shot with a rifle, but a tough one for a shotgun. Let's face it, hunting big game with a shotgun is a lot like going to bat with a broomstick in a baseball game. The implement may be

Shotgunning for whitetails has become immensely popular. The author took this nice buck in Illinois.

used somewhat effectively, but it isn't the most efficient method. But as suburbia continues its relentless sprawl into deer habitat and as humans and whitetails increasingly battle for elbowroom, more and more municipalities are mandating slug guns for hunting versus the potential next-county lethality of the modern rifle.

Nearly 3 million of the nation's 10 million whitetail deer hunters currently go afield armed with shotguns, and the number is growing every year. Ten states mandate shotgun-only hunting for deer, and 26 limit at least some of their hunters to shotguns. Pennsylvania, historic home of the American rifle, now restricts more than 100,000 of its hunters to slug guns and muzzleloaders in special-regulations areas around metropolitan areas. New York has a half-million slug shooters. Even former frontier outposts such as Helena, Montana and Edmonton, Alberta now have shotgun-only hunting areas on their outskirts.

Author with an Alabama buck which fell to a Federal slug.

Given the fast-growing market, development in slug loads and slug-shooting shotguns has advanced more in the last 20 years than any other aspect of the firearms industry. Today's high-velocity, high-tech sabot slugs and rifled-barrel slug guns have turned shotgun deer hunting from a "wait-'til-you-see-the-whites-of-their-eyes" proposition into an event where the hunter can no longer be faulted for pre-heating the oven when a rack appears a couple of hundred yards away.

Today's hunter can count on most slugs to be effective on whitetails, which wasn't always the case. In the early 1990s, when sabot slugs were still being developed, the Winchester and Federal pellet-shaped .50-caliber slugs and Remington's rugged Copper Solid shot from 12-gauge guns were very accurate but very hard— too hard to expand on deer-sized game. The result was commonly blow-throughs that didn't stagger the animals—even when they were mortally wounded—and left very poor blood trails.

I can remember the first buck I took with the newfangled sabots—a 6-pointer that passed my stand broadside at 60 yards. I put the crosshairs just behind the shoulder and confidently squeezed off a shot at the unsuspecting buck, fully expecting the "hunch-up-then-bound-30-yards" reaction common to fatal slug hits.

But this guy just stopped and looked around, obviously startled by the sound only. I'd shot the Winchester BRI slugs all summer; knew the Ithaca DeerSlayer II was very accurate. What had happened?

I immediately put the crosshairs on the same spot and fired again. Same reaction, except he took two walking strides and looked around again, his chest now covered by a tree trunk.

It had to be the scope. I must have knocked if off somehow. Now what?

Well, there was nothing to lose, so with very little confidence I pulled down on his exposed neck and pressed the trigger again. He dropped like a stone, dead before he hit the ground.

When I got to him I was shocked to see that the first two shots had hit precisely where they'd been aimed, within less than two inches of each other and through both lungs. Neither opened up or imparted any shock as they passed through his body and exited through the opposing ribs—through same-size holes. At only 1,400 fps and with a hard antimony content to keep the slugs from breaking at the wasp-waist, the slugs were too slow and too hard to expand.

The final shot killed only due to placement, breaking his neck and mercifully turning out the lights.

Obviously, I was looking for something else to hunt with the following season, and Lightfield's Hybred sabot was the answer. The New Jersey-based company's big, soft, attached-wad Hybred was the first sabot that was malleable enough to be truly effective on deer. I used it with great success on deer, bear, and caribou. In fact, it was the only sabot I hunted with until 1997 when Federal came out with the Barnes EXpander. A year later Remington's second-generation Copper Solid arrived. Now a host of high-velocity, jacketed, controlled-expansion slugs are on the market as proven deer rounds.

SLUGS: EVOLUTION AND HISTORY

Today's high-tech sabot shotgun slugs offer rifle-like ballistics— nearly 2,000 pounds of energy and uncanny accuracy at 100 yards. The ⅝-ounce, 20-gauge Foster-style slug I used to kill my first deer nearly four decades ago probably had only 600 pounds left when it found its target at 70 yards. Comparing 1960s vintage slugs with today's state-of-the-art high-velocity projectiles is like juxtaposing the Wright Brothers' Kitty Hawk flying machine and the Space Shuttle.

In my early years of slug shooting (the 1950s and '60s) virtually everyone used their rabbit guns for deer hunting. You sort of pointed slug guns in those days instead of aiming. Dad bought slugs of mixed brands from a hardware store bin at nine cents apiece. He would buy 10 new ones every year, and I would get last year's leftovers.

We paid very little attention to brands, bore sizes, even chokes. Affixing any sight system fancier than your shotgun's front bead was considered an act of conspicuous consumption. When I, as an

Early sabot slugs: Lightfield Hybred, Remington Copper Solid, Winchester BRI.

uppity teenager, put a Williams peep sight on my shotgun, I was told it was like putting racing tires on a school bus.

Accuracy has always been a relative term. In those days, a gun that would put three of five shots into a gallon can at 40 paces was a tack-driver. Today, my slug gun is a bolt-action with a heavy rifled barrel made of 4140 rifle steel. It is capable of minute-of-angle accuracy at 100 yards and is lethal at nearly 200 (under the right conditions) with slugs that are actually large-bore pistol bullets encased in a bore-filling plastic sleeve.

To adapt an advertising phrase: This is not your grandfather's slug gun. In fact, on paper, it has better ballistics than Grandpa's old rifle. Gunning magazines will tell you that the newest high-velocity slugs—the Winchester Partition Gold, Hornady H2K Heavy Mag, and Federal's high-velocity Barnes EXpander—eclipse the venerable .45–70 and other elderly centerfire calibers.

On paper, that's true. But we don't hunt on paper.

In the field, the ballistic coefficient—a figure describing a projectile's efficiency in flight using shape, length, and mass—rules a slug's potential. Today's high-tech sabot slugs may perform like rifle

Expansion is the hallmark of modern sabot slugs—Federal Barnes EXpander, Remington Copper Solid, and Lightfield Hybred.

bullets on paper, but they can't begin to compare in ballistic coefficient. That means they won't carry nearly as far or remain stable nearly as long as rifle bullets of the same velocity.

Consider that a conventional shotgun slug has a maximum range of less than 900 yards, and that's when it's fired from a barrel elevated 30 degrees. Your .30–06 will carry nearly five miles from the same position. A 10-mph crosswind will move a conventional shotgun slug 6 to 8 inches off target at 100 yards. A 130-grain bullet from a .270 fired under the same conditions will move about ⅛ inch.

Shotguns and slugs are short-range ordnance, regardless of what you may read elsewhere. Modern high-velocity shotgun slugs are effective, under the right conditions, with the right shooter, out to 125 yards. An expert might stretch it to 175 under the right conditions, but once you get much beyond 125 yards, luck has more influence on the results than ballistics.

With this in mind, sighting in a slug gun should be done at 50 yards. If you think your shots will be longer, set your groups 2.5 inches high at 50 yards—or 1 inch high with the new high-velocity sabots—and it will be dead-on at 100.

While the new stuff doesn't threaten rifle performance, it's virtually light years ahead of yesterday's slugs. Projectiles like shotgun slugs that operate in the vicinity of the sound barrier face a series of forces that rifle bullets simply fly past. Velocity, you see, has a considerable bearing on the inherent accuracy of a projectile in flight. While increased velocity is generally considered to be good, the most prominent obstacle to slug accuracy is the sonic barrier.

At sea level, in dry 65-degree air, the speed of sound is reached at 1,089 feet per second. When test pilots originally got close to the sound barrier, they had trouble keeping the aircraft flying straight. After passing the barrier, steering ability returned. The same thing happens to slugs in that velocity range. The turbulence created by the sound wave closing behind the slug as its velocity decayed to a transonic range actually buffeted older-style, less aerodynamic slugs into instability.

Not so anymore.

Prior to World War II the only slugs available were "Pumpkin Balls," semi-spherical soft lead balls that were purposely molded small enough in diameter to easily pass through any shotgun barrel, regardless of wall thickness, age, design, or choke. They were pretty much 30- to 40-yard loads.

In the early 1930s an independent ballistician named Karl Foster turned shotguns into modern-day muskets with a slug design that emulated the Minie Ball that shot so well in blackpowder rifles. Basically a molded nose-heavy lead cup with skirts that flared upon ignition to fill the bore, the Foster-style slug took over the market in the years following World War II and today—loaded by Winchester, Federal, and Remington—still serves as the bestseller nationwide.

They are called "rifled slugs" because the grooves, or flutes, swaged into the outside walls. While these grooves appear to give the slug rotation, and therefore stability in flight, a ballistician once confided to me that their main purpose was to give the surface a buffer or raised portion to squeeze down in a tight choke without disturbing the actual body of the slug. The Foster slug has a highly inefficient shape, heavy weight, and low velocity, but it stood as a vast improvement over the earlier Pumpkin Balls.

Better yet were the heavy, bore-size slugs that German Wilhelm Brenneke's shop had been producing since 1895. It was slightly modified over the years but the 2¾-inch 12-gauge version, still called the "original Brenneke" has not changed appreciably since 1935. Due to a couple of World Wars, this German invention didn't get much exposure on our own shores until the 1950s. Today, they stand with the Fosters as the prime ordnance for smoothbore guns.

Thus, with some minor alterations, slug shooting remained virtually the same from the 1930s through the mid-1980s. But the advent of sabot slugs and rifled barrels accelerated slug development to warp speed.

Adapting an artillery design, slug makers started building "sabot" slugs—smaller diameter, more aerodynamic slugs—and encased them in bore-filling, fall-away plastic sleeves. This allowed the ballistically cavernous shotgun bore to throw a much more efficient projectile, and the plastic sleeves grabbed the rifling and imparted a stabilizing spin on the whole unit.

The earliest commercial design came out of California and BRI (Ballistic Research Industries) labs, which used a .50-caliber, 1-ounce wasp-waisted pellet with a hollow rear (plugged with a wooden dowel) loaded in a two-piece polyethylene sleeve. Smith & Wesson at one point marketed them as police loads (they'd shoot through engine blocks or car and house doors with little deflection) and quickly relabeled them to sell to the hunting market as well. Winchester bought the BRI patent in 1990 and the next year Federal Cartridge brought out a higher-velocity but visually identical model based on an older BRI patent.

The design was very accurate but much too hard to expand on deer-size game and was markedly slower than fullbore slugs—

This Remington Copper Solid was recovered from a 250-pound bear.

putting it at a distinct disadvantage for the short-range shooting typical of whitetail hunting. The sabot's true advantage came farther downrange where the combination of spin and nose-heavy design kept it stable past 100 yards—retaining its energy well past the point where the fullbore slugs had petered out.

The tiny Lightfield Ammunition Corporation was formed to produce a design formulated by British designer Tony Kinchin—the first expanding saboted slug. The Lightfield was actually much closer to the 3-inch Brenneke design, or the similar Activ attached-wad design, but encased in a two-piece thin sabot.

The Lightfield was a full 547 grains (an ounce and a quarter) of very soft lead with a diameter of 0.670, which needed little to bring it to bore size. Activ Industries in West Virginia originally loaded the Lightfields, but that work went to Hungary when Activ ran into financial hardship in the mid-1990s.

Brenneke didn't stand still. Soon after rifled-barrel guns became available it became apparent that the Brenneke design's high fins were easily destroyed by rifling, making them incompatible with rifled bores.

To get a foothold in the new market Brenneke introduced the 600-grain Golden Slug in 1993, just as Ithaca Gun brought out its fast-twist (one turn in 25 inches) DeerSlayer II to accommodate the big slug. (See "Making Your Slug Gun Shoot Better" later in this chapter for further details on rate of twist.)

Next in the slam-bang development of slugs came Remington's revolutionary Copper Solid—a 1-ounce, .50-caliber slug with an open, slotted nose that was machined out of solid copper bar stock. Machining rather than a pressurized molding (swaging), made the slugs much more consistent, and the Copper Solid was a huge developmental lunge forward in that it was the first rear-weighted slug. It was, in fact, a bullet.

Manufacturers had, until then, been extremely careful to stay away from any designs that looked or acted like bullets—the symbol that politically-correct legislators were working against. But when no serious repercussions followed, slug manufacturers began trotting out actual bullets to be loaded in shotgun sabots. The first breakthrough was the 1996 introduction of a .50-caliber Randy Brooks soft copper Barnes X-Bullet loaded in a 12-gauge Fiocchi hull. The load was devised by small New Jersey-based innovator Chris Youngs under his Gun Servicing Collet Cup Magnum label.

The next year Federal Cartridge followed with Premium load called the Barnes EXpander based on a similar Barnes X-Bullet that was built on a proprietary basis for Federal. The bullet, which was fired at conventional sabot velocities—1,400 to 1,500 fps at the muzzle—expanded more than 100 percent and typically retained 100 percent of its mass on deer.

Remington, which had run into problems with its ultra-hard original Copper Solid, redesigned it to match the Federal load in 1998. Meanwhile, Winchester-Olin had been working on a project of its own for three years, using a version of the Partition Gold bullet it had used for pistol and muzzleloader loads. A product of Winchester's

Combined Technologies effort with Nosler, the Partition Gold was a specially jacketed lead-core bullet that sat on a partition and was filled with a lead tail—a design that controls yet accentuates expansion.

The bullet was 385 grains compared to the 440-grain norm for conventional sabots (and expanders) and had a uniquely high (for slugs) ballistic coefficient of 0.220. Consider that the average Foster slug's ballistic coefficient is around 0.060, and the super-accurate Winchester Hi-Impact and Federal Premium sabots were about 0.101.

But pushing the new slug to high velocity was a problem for Winchester because the higher pressure tended to wrap the sabot around the slug, hampering its release. Finally, designers found that by molding an aluminum floor into the plastic sabot for the slug to rest on, the combination would be stiff enough to perform under higher chamber pressure.

The Winchester Supreme Partition Gold slug burst onto the market with a great deal of hype and was a tremendous retail success, selling out its production runs almost immediately even at a considerably higher retail than any other slug. The new slug showed extraordinary terminal ballistics, extremely flat trajectory at a projected 1,900 fps muzzle velocity, and 3,200 foot-pounds of energy at the muzzle.

Winchester's "star" sabot and its Partition Gold slug.

It would have been unique had Hornady not revamped its first failed effort at slug making, the ATP, into the high-velocity H2K Heavy Mag, a Hornady controlled-expansion bullet loaded to a muzzle velocity of 2,000 fps.

High velocity has become the goal of current slug makers. Lightfield introduced the uniquely designed 3- and 3.5-inch Commander series recently, which projects muzzle velocities of 1,800 and 1,900 fps for 500-grain slugs. The Commander's sabot actually remains attached until it penetrates the target, rather than flying off en route. Not only does the design eliminate the ballistic nightmare of shedding the sabot, but it also stiffens the load to withstand the increased chamber pressure that comes with higher velocity.

Brenneke also has devised its own high-velocity load, the Super Sabot, which incorporates a sliding copper sleeve over a soft-nosed aluminum projectile. The new load is available in both 2¾- and 3-inch 12-gauge versions with a top muzzle velocity of 1,640 fps.

Federal, not wanting to fall behind in the slug market, introduced a high-velocity version of its Premium Barnes EXpander, projecting 1,900 fps with a 325-grain Barnes X-Bullet slug (actually the slug loaded in its 20-gauge EXpander for two years) in a 12-gauge configuration.

In 2002, Winchester came right back with the Platinum Tip sabot slug, an adaptation of the company's FailSafe bullet design — essentially a .50-caliber Black Talon pistol bullet with a silver jacket rather than the brand's customary black. The Platinum Tip is, at 400 grains, slightly heavier and, at 1,700 fps, slightly slower than the Partition Gold. It is also slightly less expensive and is specifically designed to perform on deer-size game.

At the same time Lightfield came out with a low-velocity, low-recoil 2¾-inch 12-gauge round called Lightfield Lites, and Remington stepped back into the fray with the Core-Lokt Ultra bonded slug, a 1,900 fps, 385-grain, .50-caliber version of its popular rifle ammo line, as well as a Brenneke-style, attached-wad 500-grain lead slug it calls the Buck Hammer.

Big Green also juiced up its rifled slug line with a high-velocity (1,700 fps) Slugger, which is actually a reintroduction of the company's ⅞-ounce slug that was discontinued in favor of a 1-ounce version in the early 1980s.

No matter how you look at it, slug shooting has come a long way, baby. And it doesn't look like that evolution will end any time soon.

CORRECT HANDLING OF SLUGS

Temperature and moisture have profound effects on slug performance. I've seen slugs stored in a drafty shed over the winter that have lost more than 300 feet per second when fired the next spring. Not only do atmospheric conditions affect powder, but plastic hulls (roll crimps) and sabots (dimensions) also change with temperature and humidity.

The garage, woodshed, or barn is definitely not the place to store slugs. Even if they've been stored correctly in a sealed container, if they are opened and left in the trunk of your car for a few days, the ballistic characteristics are bound to change.

Shotgun slugs, with the exception of the Hornady H2K (second from right), have "a hole in the roof"—the exposed slug and roll crimp allows moisture into the hull.

But if you have a batch of slugs that gets fouled, don't throw them out or give them to your no-account brother-in-law. Slug expert Randy Fritz says that taking them into a climate-controlled setting (your house should do) for a few weeks will likely dry them out enough to perform well again. Keeping them in the house during the winter, where the temperature is relatively constant and the humidity is low, is ideal. But what do you do when the humidity of spring and summer hits?

"After they are dried out, I'd suggest packing them in air-tight covers—Zip-Loc bags are fine—and storing them in a cheap cooler with a tight lid," says Fritz. "I keep them in that kind of storage year-round. And don't forget to maintain that kind of situation in hunting season, too.

"If you're carrying them in your pocket, or a pack, or—worse yet—one of those bands on the stock, they're absorbing moisture," says Fritz. "If you get wet, it's just common sense that they're wet, too."

Granted, if you're only shooting at a buck from 40 to 50 yards, the difference in performance isn't likely to be noticeable. But there will be a difference, nevertheless. If your slugs lose or gain 300 feet per second in velocity, it translates to thousands of pounds in chamber pressure. A shift of 2,000 to 3,000 foot-pounds in a rifle, where chamber pressure is 50,000 to 60,000 foot-pounds, is inconsequential. Make a shift that size in a shotgun chamber, where pressure is usually less than 12,000 foot-pounds, and the percentage of loss is significant—sometimes translating to several inches difference in elevation 100 yards downrange.

Slugs are loaded under controlled conditions of extremely low humidity and high temperature, making them "hot" ballistically. The reasoning is that the slugs will take on moisture during shipping and storage, and velocity will fall into the specified range.

Store your slugs properly and you should get the performance you want.

SPECIALIZED SLUG GUNS

The rifled-barrel slug gun is state of the art and all major shotgun manufacturers—Remington, Mossberg, U.S. Repeating Arms, Browning, Ithaca, H&R, Marlin, Savage, Beretta, and Benelli—offer at least one model with a rifled barrel. Although smoothbore shotguns and conventional slugs still make up more than half of the retail market, rifled barrels and sabot slugs are the most advanced and accurate and represent the fastest growing segment of the industry.

Not surprisingly, the evolution of the shotgun slug led the technological improvement of the slug-shooting shotgun. Slugs were thrown through conventional smoothbore barrels with bead sights almost exclusively until Ithaca Gun made a bold move in 1959. The company, based in the shotgun-only country of upstate New York, that year introduced the DeerSlayer—a variation of the Model 37 bottom-ejection pump that featured an extremely tight (0.704 inches as opposed to the industry 12-gauge standard of 0.730) barrel with no forcing cones or choke, topped with rifle sights.

Author with a Browning Gold Hunter, a state-of-the-art autoloading slug gun.

Ithaca's Storm DeerSlayer II is the newest version of the company's 1937 pump design.

Unencumbered by choke and squeezed tightly to seal the gases behind it, the rifled slugs of the day flew amazingly straight out of the new Ithaca innovation. It was a dedicated slug gun in that it would not pattern shot efficiently at all with no choke or forcing cone.

The next big move in slug guns came in 1987 when both Ithaca and Mossberg introduced rifled-barrel versions of the DeerSlayer and Model 500, respectively. The rifling was designed to grip the sabot sleeves of the then-new BRI-style sabot, opening a whole new world of accuracy and effective range.

You'll find that today's dedicated slug guns have short, 20- to 22-inch barrels. That's because the powders used to propel most shotgun slugs are burned in the first 16 or 17 inches of barrel length, so any barrel of at least 18 inches should be adequate in that respect.

The Tar-Hunt RSG-12 is custom made by Pennsylvanian Randy Fritz.

The state of the art in slug guns is the bolt action. Once the least-expensive, simplest shotgun action, the addition of the rifled barrel and a few other amenities (like fiber-optic sights, rifle-style synthetic stocks, and scope mounts) has turned the bolt from a beginner's gun into the most inherently accurate slug gun available.

Mossberg's 695 and the Savage 210F Master Shot are the only commercial bolt-action guns, with suggested retail prices in the $300-$400 range, which means they can often be found through dealers for $50-$100 less. Both feature synthetic stocks and are available only in 12-gauge, with no 20-gauge plans in the future.

Marlin's 512 was the first-ever bolt-action, rifled-barrel gun, starting off in 1994 as essentially a Marlin 55 goose gun with a rifled barrel and checkered stock. (The model was discontinued due to slumping sales in 2001.) The Browning A-Bolt slug gun, essentially the company's bolt-action rifle design chambered for 12-gauge, was probably the best-built production slug gun ever made, but it enjoyed only a short lifespan, being discontinued in 1998 after just three years of production. The gun sold for more than twice the price of the Mossberg and Marlin bolts, and consumers just weren't willing to pay the difference.

Tar-Hunt Rifles of Bloomsburg, Pennsylvania makes 12- and 20-gauge bolt-action slug guns with Remington 700-like actions, McMillian synthetic stocks, and Jewell triggers. They retail for $1,795 to $2,000.

The bolt action is accurate because the barrel is fixed (screwed) to the receiver and the entire function of the gun is in a straight line (meaning no load levering up from below while the empty is being ejected, as in an autoloader), which means less barrel-shaking, accuracy-robbing vibration. That's a major factor in shotguns, which recoil nearly ⅝ inch before the projectile leaves the barrel.

Single-shot, break-open slug guns such as the H&R 980 and 925 Ultra Slugster (bull-barreled 12- and 20-gauge models) and

This fine buck was taken with a Tar-Hunt slug gun and Lightfield Commander.

Mossberg's 12-gauge SSI-One are similarly accurate but tend to be heavier and lack the quick follow-up of the bolt actions. Because the scope rail is mounted directly on the chamber, these guns also tend to be rougher on scopes.

Pumps are the most popular slug guns, probably due to retail price, as well as their light weight, durability, and simplicity. The compact, lightweight aspect of the pump makes it the darling of the still-hunter as well as hunters using treestands or blinds. Follow-up shots are easier with a pump than with any action other than an autoloader, but heavier recoil is the price you pay.

There are nearly 10 million Remington 12-, 16-, and 20-gauge 870s wandering around the country, while the 12-gauge Mossberg 500 and 835 Ultri-Mag are among the sales leaders every year. Ithaca's M37 pump comes in several gauge configurations (12, 16, and 20) for deer hunters, including the 11-pound, 12-gauge bull-barreled Deer-

Slayer III, which is available only by special order through the company. The newly revamped company also introduced the Ithaca Storm in 2002, a synthetic-stocked, Parkerized version of its longstanding DeerSlayer II, which features a fixed rifled barrel. The Storm, at $399 suggested retail, is $200 cheaper than the earlier versions. The Browning BPS (12-gauge), Winchester 1300 (12- and 20-gauge), and the 12-gauge Benelli Nova all are also offered in rifled-barrel versions.

Double-barreled shotguns, be they side-by-sides or over-unders, are notoriously inaccurate for slug shooting because both bores usually have their own point of aim. For that reason, no doubles are currently made with rifled barrels.

The autoloader is popular due to its quick follow-ups and tendency toward lessened recoil. The trade-off is that they are generally much heavier and far more expensive than other actions. They are also more complicated and often less reliable and somewhat less accurate due to the excessive vibration caused by the cycling action.

The Remington 1100 is the lightest and oldest autoloading model on the market, and it is available in both 12- and 20-gauge slug versions. It's a longtime favorite with slug hunters, as is its successor, the 12-gauge 11–87. Browning's Gold (12 and 20), Benelli's 12-gauge Super Black Eagle and M1, Beretta's 12-gauge ES100 (formerly the Pintail), and Traditions' Spanish-built autoloader are all popular with slug hunters in both rifled barrels and smoothbores. Mossberg's 9200 also fit that bill until it was discontinued in 2000.

The Mossberg 695 is the best-selling bolt-action slug gun.

MAKING YOUR SLUG GUN SHOOT BETTER

What about accuracy in a slug gun? One-inch groups at 100 yards have been achieved by expert shooters with custom guns and saboted slugs under the right conditions. In the everyday world, with commercial ordnance and a weekend shooter, you'll find that anything inside five inches at 100 yards is asking a lot of an out-of-the-box production slug gun. A slug gun and load that groups 2 to 3 inches at 100 yards is a tack-driver.

The good news is that virtually any shotgun can be made to perform better. In fact, almost all of them can be substantially improved. The first consideration in improving your slug gun is the barrel. If you shoot a smoothbore shotgun, don't bother with sabot loads. They are designed to be shot through rifled barrels and will not perform well out of a smoothbore—without spinning, the sabots

Lifting the comb makes it easier to see through the scope and reduces felt recoil.

aren't likely to shed efficiently and accuracy will suffer. Besides, they cost five to seven times more than conventional slugs.

Rifled slugs or non-sabot attached-wad slugs (Original Brenneke, Brenneke K.O., Fiocchi, Activ, Challenger, and so on) are designed for smoothbore guns and work well, albeit with less effective range than sabot slugs in rifled barrels.

If you have a smoothbore and want to profit from the sabot slug's longer effective range, simply fit your gun with a rifled choke tube. While a 2- to 5-inch rifled tube isn't likely to be as efficient as a fully rifled barrel, it is a low-cost option. Although some rifled choke tubes shoot well to 75 or 80 yards, common sense should tell you that imparting a 40,000 rpm spin on a slug that has already reached terminal velocity when it hits the rifling is a lot less effective than spinning it from the chamber.

Slugs have a tendency to tilt slightly in the forcing cones of conventional smoothbore guns and are potentially squeezed or deformed by tight chokes, which has an obvious effect on accuracy. But modern larger-diameter rifled slugs, and other attached-wad fullbore slugs make that far less of a problem than it was 20 years ago. Today's slugs may be shot through full choke or less, although guns with more open chokes generally throw better groups. Backbored guns, however, are not conducive to accurate slug shooting because the slug can't efficiently seal the bore, resulting in gases blowing past, lower pressure and velocity, and generally poor consistency.

Your other alternative is an aftermarket rifled barrel. Hastings has pretty much dominated the rifled-barrel aftermarket since it entered in the mid-1980s and has since expanded its line to provide French-made rifled Paradox barrels for virtually all common shotguns. All aftermarket barrels are easily interchangeable with factory barrels, with no gunsmithing required.

Next, make sure the twist rate is right for your particular load. The latest research shows a fast twist (1-turn-in-25-inches or 1-in-28

Pinning the barrel to the receiver can improve accuracy.

available from Ithaca, Browning, Winchester, Benelli, Beretta, Franchi, or Marlin) stabilizes saboted ammunition best, while 1-in-34 rates are the best compromise for sabots and short fullbore slugs. A slow twist like 1-in-36 is ideal if you're shooting only fullbore slugs. Most 20-gauge barrels have 1-in-24 to 1-in-28 twist.

To my way of thinking, the next step in improving performance for a slug gun is to lighten and stiffen the trigger. Even if your gun is a "buck special" with rifle sights and maybe a rifled barrel, it's going to have the same receiver, internal mechanisms, and trigger mechanism as its counterpart designed for scatter shot. A shotgun trigger is designed to be slapped, not squeezed like a rifle trigger. And the insurance carriers for gun companies like to see substantial creep in triggers that are also set for a hearty slap.

I don't care if you're the type who can crush cue balls with your fist, nobody can wring full potential out of a firearm with an 8- to

10-pound trigger pull. In a perfect world, we'd have slug guns with crisp 3- to 3.5-pound pulls, but in this world even a 5- or 6-pounder isn't bad so long as there's no creep.

You're going to find that many of the factors that need attention to make your slug gun shoot better are also things that trapshooters work with. That's why I look at publications that cater to trapshooters—*Shotgun Sports* magazine and shooting sports supply outlets like Gamaliel (www.gamaliel.com)—to find items and gunsmithing services for slug shooting.

For instance, both slug shooters and trapshooters want to lessen recoil and barrel jump. There are a variety of recoil-reduction devices for shotguns that answer those needs. Mercury-filled tubes (often called Dead Mules) that can be inserted in the stock or forearm of your shotgun are very effective at suppressing recoil. There are also a variety of specialty recoil pads to add to the effectiveness.

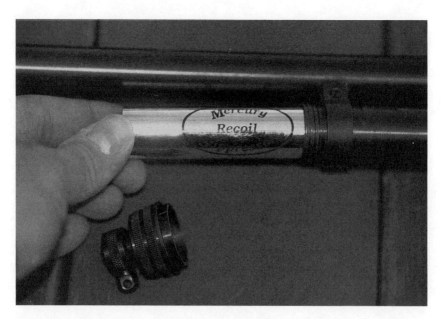

A recoil reduction device can be an aid to accuracy.

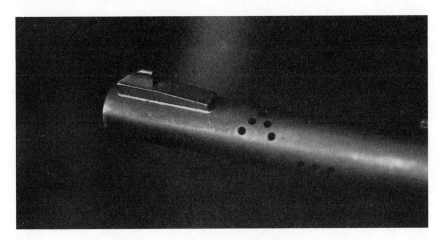

Porting the barrel reduces muzzle jump, lessens felt recoil, and increases the auditory effect of the muzzle blast.

Barrel porting reduces felt recoil and muzzle jump while also having the effect of disturbing muzzle gases and allowing sabots to break away freely. Porting, crown polishing, and the aforementioned trigger work and barrel pinning may be beyond the work of a local gunsmith. But gunsmiths and companies advertising in trapshooting publications will know what you're talking about and what you need—and they'll be experienced in doing the work.

So don't be discouraged about the performance (or lack thereof) of your current slug gun. The bad news is that right out of the box most slug guns won't be tack-drivers. But the good news is that most all of them can be made to shoot better.

SIGHTING YOUR SLUG GUN

Shooting a slug gun from a bench is a brutal, bone-jarring, teeth-rattling, ear-ringing, humbling experience. But it also takes finesse, experience, and more than a little know-how to shoot accurately and get dependable results.

So how should a slug gun be tested or sighted in? First, let's put egos aside and admit that as much as we all like to think of ourselves as pretty fair marksmen, pinpoint 100-yard target accuracy is simply not readily achievable by the average hunter, regardless of the slug or gun. There are simply too many variables involved in shooting for the average shooter to honestly define the accuracy of a particular barrel or load by simply squeezing off a few rounds.

The biggest variable is, of course, the shooter. Today's slugs are more accurate than most shooters. For example, we know that race-cars can run laps in excess of 230 mph at the Indianapolis Speedway, but 99 percent of American drivers couldn't get the polesitter's car past 120 mph without crashing. It's the same with shooting. There are a few true experts who have the experience and ability to wring the last ounce of potential out of a gun and/or load. The rest of us rely on various degrees of approximation and luck.

When shooting a slug gun off a bench, be sure to grip the forearm and pull it downward.

Even when you're experienced it's possible to mess up. I shoot more rounds in a year than the average hunter does in a lifetime, yet my technique is still the first suspect when a gun or load isn't grouping well. Many is the time a load wouldn't tighten inside of three inches at 50 yards and I would be on the verge of writing it off as just another hollow claim. Then I'd make a minor technique adjustment and put the next several shots in one hole.

Other variables? Well, one big one would be the rest. Is it solid? Can you make minute adjustments without torquing the barrel? Is the forearm rest soft enough to absorb the initial vibration at ignition? No, a rolled-up jacket on the truck hood isn't a good enough rest. You need a steady bench, and it pays to have a solid, adjustable rifle rest and rear bag.

A shotgun recoils nearly ⅛ inch while the slug is still in the barrel and any vibration can affect accuracy. Even a loose magazine cap can throw slugs off by a couple of inches at 100 yards. Imagine the effect of resting a pumpgun on its slide when you shoot. The receiver of a pump should rest on the bag, not the forearm or slide.

Good shooting is more than a good position on the bench and a general knowledge of the sight picture, though. It takes practice to apply the same gradually increasing pressure to the trigger until the breaking point is reached on each shot.

Here are some guidelines for shooting slug guns off a bench:

- Use a quality rear bag and line the recoil pad of the gun directly over the back edge of the bag.
- Keep the front sling stud two inches forward of the front bag.
- Pull back firmly on the pistol grip with the right hand.
- Use the left hand (just behind the rest) to pull the forearm downward and rearward at the same time.

We've all seen experts shooting rifles off benches with the gun's forearm lying on the front bag and the shooter's left hand tucked in front of him on the bench. But those guys aren't shooting 600-grain loads. Tuck that left hand underneath when shooting a slug gun off a bench and you're likely to be using it next to wipe a bloody brow. A 7-pound, 12-gauge slug gun exerts approximately the same felt recoil as a .300 magnum rifle, and a thin-walled shotgun barrel kicks more wildly than a sleek rifle barrel.

How about the range? Do you use wind flags? Yes, a breeze is a factor even with full-ounce projectiles. A big factor. A 440-grain saboted slug will move more than half a foot from the point of aim at 100 yards with a 10-mph crosswind. Fosters wander even more.

Okay, you know the routine. You know your gun. It's a dead-calm day and you're still not satisfied with how the gun groups. Keep in mind that if a commercial slug gun puts three shots in a 4-inch group at 100 yards it's probably performing within the specs set by the manufacturer. Minute-of-angle slugs and slug guns—those that

Sight in slug guns at 50 yards and make adjustments accordingly.

will shoot a 1-inch group at 100 yards—are extreme rarities, regardless of what you read in magazines.

But let's also understand that 100-yard target accuracy isn't essential to the average slug hunter. Most of our shots are well inside of 80 yards at vital areas nearly twice the diameter of a basketball; a difference of an inch or two at 100 yards is moot.

One concession the average slug shooter should make is to shoot 50-yard ranges rather than 100. The human variable is magnified appreciably in that second 50 yards, making it much harder to make accurate judgments. If you're shooting sabots with the correct twist rate, once you get a combination shooting in the same hole at 50 yards, rest assured it will group well at 100. If you're grouping fullbore slugs well at 50, count on similar groups out to 75–80 yards.

And be happy with that.

OPTICS FOR SHOTGUNS

In my formative years as a slug shooter, our deer guns were simply our rabbit guns with different loads. A front bead on the barrel was the extent of the aiming system. If you remembered to get your head down tight enough on the stock to look down the barrel on a level with the bead, you might have been able to hit a pie plate at 40 yards. Maybe.

As slugs improved, more and more manufacturers came out with "buck specials"—the same shotguns only with buckhorn rifle sights instead of the lone bead. But the fact remains that open sights simply will not allow the shooter to aim precisely enough to take full advantage of the accuracy of modern sophisticated loads and barrels—so shooters have turned to fiber optics.

Optics on a shotgun? Honestly, it was virtually unheard of until recently. In the deer or turkey woods, optics are a godsend to anyone with failing vision or even a skewed barrel. Barrels or chokes that don't shoot directly to point of aim are common among today's

Every scope manufacturer now makes at least one model specifically for shotguns.

shotguns, a situation that can be righted by adjusting a sighting device to compensate.

Be advised that an inexpensive rifle scope isn't the answer for slug or turkey guns. Shotguns don't contain their concussion in the receiver like rifles do, so they punish a scope more than a rifle would. A $39.95 Blue Light Special isn't likely to last long in the woods.

It takes a good quality scope to resist shotgun punishment, and the shooter is wise to use one that is designed specifically for shotguns. Most companies are making their shotgun scopes parallax-free at 50 to 75 yards rather than 100 to 150 yards like rifle scopes. And they are built along much more sturdy lines. (If you move your head—with a stationary scope and gun—and the dot stays on the bull's-eye regardless of your head position, the scope is said to be parallax-free.)

One drawback to shotgun-only scopes is that they tend to be of low magnification with a small objective lens. That means you lose

More and more big game and turkey hunters are now opting for optics like this Pentax Lightseeker in Mossy Oak camo.

precious minutes locking on a target in low-light conditions. Leupold, Nikon, and a few other companies do, however, offer 2X to 7X variable shotgun scopes with a larger objective lens, and Sightron has a fixed 4-power with a large objective.

While a cheap rifle scope is a bad idea for a shotgun, a good quality rifle scope will stand up to the added punishment. Most high-end or upper mid-range rifle scopes ($250 and up) are tested to withstand the recoil of a .375 magnum rifle and should stand up to the abuse a shotgun imparts. It won't be parallax-free at close range, but that's a very minor factor that most shooters won't even notice.

My rule of thumb is that a shooter should pay as much, if not more, for a scope than he does for the shotgun. The gun, after all, is only as effective as the optics. If they don't work well, the gun is useless.

Magnification for either a slug gun or turkey gun in most instances is a matter of personal preference. For most hunters a 4X is good for a hunting slug gun, but target shooters may opt for more magnification. Turkey hunters may want something with little or no magnification, with 2X the high end. Magnification may help failing eyes to identify birds and beard length, but it can be confusing when it comes to estimating distance.

Illuminated-dot electronic sighting devices—virtually standard in combat-style pistol competitions—have also found a home with slug and turkey hunters. The Swedish-made Aimpoint celebrated its

Aimpoint was the first illuminated-dot scope on the market. Nowadays virtually all optics manufacturers offer at least one such model.

25th anniversary at the turn of the century, although it didn't reach America as the first illuminated-dot sighting device until 1981. It is still the industry leader, even though virtually every other major optics manufacturer has a version of its own.

When buying an electronic-dot sight, check to make sure that it is parallax-free, an important consideration. Also consider that under some conditions, such as dim light (dusk or dawn), the dot, regardless of how low you adjust the illumination, will be so bright that it will darken the screen and keep you from aiming. With a snowy background or in bright conditions, the illuminated-dot sights are terrific.

Always use steel (not aluminum) scope rings for shotguns, as they will stand up to the punishment. When mounting scopes on shotguns or magnum rifles, I like to add a drop of contact cement to the rings to lock the scope tube in place, particularly if the rings have been lapped for a good fit.

Shotguns under glass are a relatively new but necessary concept that will only improve as more and more shooters opt for optics.

WHAT ABOUT BUCKSHOT?

Buckshot has been a popular and effective load since blackpowder days and is still the load mandated for deer hunting in specific areas of at least 10 states. It's legal in 29 states, although five of them don't have any whitetails.

Like all shotgun loads, buckshot has improved markedly in the last couple of decades. Shotcup development, copper plating, improved lead-antimony mixes, and granulated plastic buffering have turned the once willy-nilly patterning characteristics of buckshot into an even more devastating tool.

Previously, users of No. 00 (double-aught) buckshot found patterns extremely ragged at close range—to the point where a deer-size target might be missed altogether at 40 yards. Like any shotgun

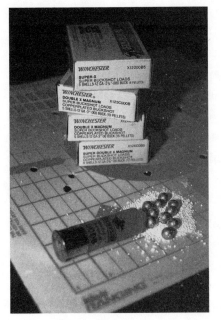

Buckshot comes in a variety of sizes.

scatter load, the problem is that the bigger the pellet (00 pellets are .33 caliber) the less room it has to negotiate in the crowded confines of a shotgun bore. Backbored barrels will give demonstrably better patterning than conventional diameter barrels with smaller pellets. In the old days, the majority of the soft, unplated pellets were damaged or worn by the barrel walls as they sorted themselves out en route to the muzzle.

Because of this, many buckshot hunters in those days opted for smaller shot such as No. 4 (.24 caliber), which patterned much denser than the larger shot. The lethality of No. 4 shot, however, is questionable beyond 20–30 yards.

If you talked to old-time buckshot hunters full choke was the only logical choice. But with today's improved choke systems, and with the plastic sleeves and buffer keeping the shot from being deformed in the barrel, good patterns can be obtained with modified or even improved cylinder choking. New loads, including the relatively new No. 000 (.36-caliber pellets), are more effective than ever in open-choke guns for the same reason.

With today's loads, effective patterning ranges have lengthened appreciably. For instance, No. 00 today, fired through a full-choke, 12-gauge barrel, would probably average 50 percent (6 of 12 pellets) in the traditional patterning target of a 30-inch circle at 70 yards. Just 10 years ago a 50-percent pattern could be achieved at no farther than 40 yards. But please note that I'm talking about "effective patterning ranges." This is certainly not an endorsement of 70-yard shots with buckshot.

Back to patterning. While a 30-inch pattern is a fine criterion for wingshooting birds, we're aiming at a 12- to 16-inch vital area on a deer. A pie plate is a better target.

I took to the range recently with a Browning Auto-5 and an Ithaca Model 87, with interchangeable (but different make) choke tubes and a box full of Winchester 2¾- and 3-inch No. 00 and No.

Examples of buckshot patterns at various ranges.

000 buckshot loads. In an extended testing session with both guns it was clear that the No. 00 buck wouldn't reliably put more than eight of its pellets in a pie-plate-size target at 30 yards. With some choke constrictions I didn't even get four pellets in the target. Some loads liked full choke, others improved cylinder, and I found that just a tiny change in constriction could make a dramatic difference in pattern density.

Differences in the length of forcing cones in various guns and in barrel and choke diameters or whether a gun is backbored are all going to make a dramatic difference in how a particular load performs. Finding out how various buckshot loads perform in your own shotgun before heading into the woods is essential.

I've hunted deer in areas that mandated the use of shotguns all my life, a few times where buckshot was *de rigueur*. And I've been successful with buckshot and have no horror stories to relate about wounded animals or missed opportunities, but one day of range testing convinced me that my success was as much a case of good fortune as it was prime (read short-ranged) opportunity.

Buckshot is well-known as a very potent short-range load.

Sure, buckshot loads are now better than ever, but as far as I'm concerned anything beyond 35 yards is a definite "maybe." Remington's 2003 introduction of Hevi-Shot buckshot may change all this, but right now buckshot is most effective within basic archery range. And with some load-choke combinations, 20 yards might be too far.

Every time I do a shotgun seminar I hear a few stories of buckshot bringing down bucks with 60- or 80-yard shots. Yes, it can be done. But I'd never suggest it, and ethical hunters shouldn't condone it. Given the rapidity with which a single, semi-round pellet slows (and thus sheds its energy), I have to say that the aforementioned 35-yard envelope is based more on ballistic surety than a luckily-placed pellet.

If you have to shoot buckshot, do your homework. No relative, neighbor, outdoor writer, or store clerk can accurately tell you what load(s) your gun and choke will handle best. You'll probably be surprised how badly some sizes perform and how well others do. Try a variety of shot sizes (No. 00 is probably the most versatile and effective) and a variety of chokes (extended chokes seem to outperform

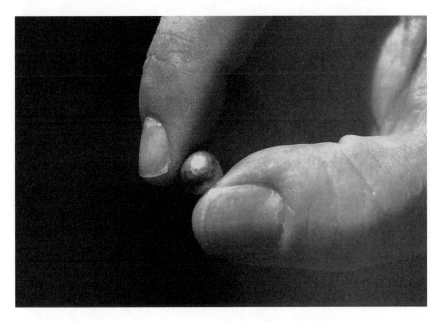

Buckshot's effectiveness comes from the cumulative clout of its pellets.

conventional screw-ins) before making a decision. And remember when patterning that a 10-inch circle is a far better judge of buckshot effectiveness than the traditional 30-inch circle.

Also remember that regardless of pattern density a buckshot pellet has the ballistic coefficient of a bowling ball. It loses energy and effectiveness very quickly. With most loads, if you are shooting beyond 40 yards your hopes of success are based on a very lucky strike from a stray pellet—definitely not an ethical shot.

Buckshot comes in seven sizes for a 12-gauge: No. 000 (10 pellets, .36 caliber in 3-inch shell); No. 00 (15 pellets, .33 caliber in 3-inch and 12 pellets in 2¾-inch shell); No. 0 (12 pellets, .32 caliber in 2¾-inch shell); No. 1 (20 pellets, .30 caliber in 2¾-inch shell, 24 in 3-inch shell); No. 2 (25 pellets, .27 caliber in 2¾-inch shell); No. 3 (32 pellets, .25 caliber in 2¾-inch shell); and No. 4 (41 pellets, .24 caliber in 3-inch shell, 34 pellets in 2¾-inch). The number of pellets may vary with the manufacturer. American shotshell manufacturers usually reserve No. 2 and 4 shot for 20-gauge loads.

Buckshot is, and always has been, an effective load for deer hunting, but only in the hands of those who know and abide by the load's limited effectiveness.

DEER HUNTING TECHNIQUES

Whitetail hunters in the East, South, and Midwest commonly hunt one of three ways: from elevated treestands or ground blinds, still-hunting slowly through woodlots, or participating in a deer drive with men or dogs (where legal). These techniques often involve short-range shooting, and shotguns make great choices for each style of hunting.

Let's take a look at each method through some specific situations encountered afield.

STAND HUNTING

I had just arranged myself in the treestand and untied the slug gun from the hoist string and loaded it when movement caught my eye. At first it was just a shadow moving through the brush, then it began to take form—then antlers materialized. The young 8-pointer was feeding his way through the dim light, dawn still a pink hint on the horizon. He was moving toward a thicket to the north where he would bed for the day.

My 15-foot-high aerie afforded me the height to see over the underbrush, but only a here-and-there glimpse of the deer as he moved through the saplings. Experience told me where he was headed and that I had to pick an opening ahead of him and wait for him to step into it.

It was only about 75 yards, but the opening was small and, after all, this was a slug gun. Just as his front shoulder hit the opening I grunted and he stopped. It was the only break I needed, the crosshairs already on his vitals.

The stand hunter can use virtually any action he prefers, and gun weight isn't much of a consideration.

At the sound of the shot he gave the definitive mule-kick, loped about 30 yards, and piled up, his white belly hair flashing his whereabouts in the brush.

The stand hunter generally wants a short-barreled gun, which is easier to handle from the perch. I was using a short (no receiver) 9-pound H&R 980 bull-barreled, single-shot 12-gauge since weight is not as much of a factor to the stand hunter, nor is action. I needed accuracy, which that gun provides, especially when topped with a decent scope to discern openings in thick brush.

From a stand the hunter is more likely to encounter animals that aren't aware of his presence, thus the shots will often be more deliberate. If the stand is in the woods, choice of load, or even gauge, isn't usually critical, either. The velocity and construction of the slug make very little difference in the close-range shooting typically found in a woodlot.

Treestands, however, are not always situated in woodlots. On a recent hunt in Arkansas, I was in a morning stand over an irrigation ditch that separated me from a brushy hedgerow lining a 40-acre sorghum field. The height of the stand allowed me to see over the brush and into the field, where a column of does soon strode into view at what I quickly judged to be about 80 yards.

I put the crosshairs on the biggest doe and squeezed off a shot with the 20-gauge Browning Gold Hunter. She stopped, looked around, and made an obviously healthy retreat to the brush, along with her horde.

The gun shot Winchester's Platinum Tip slugs very well, and I was confident of the trigger squeeze. But there was no doubt that the slug missed her by so much that she was reacting to the report of the gun rather than a near miss. Being the type of guy who reads the directions only after getting stumped, I then pulled out the laser rangefinder and quickly determined that the doe I'd judged to be 80 yards distant was actually 122 yards away.

Careful, patient still-hunters with the right shotgun and load don't come home empty-handed.

About a half-hour later another big doe—possibly the same one emboldened by my previous display of marksmanship—sauntered out in roughly the same area. Adjusting the sight picture slightly based on my new knowledge of the yardage, I dumped her with one shot.

If your stand overlooks cropland or a sizeable field where longer shots may be necessary, as in the previous scenario, a high-velocity slug (12-, 16-, or 20-gauge) that shoots flatter becomes more useful, particularly when matched up with suitable optics.

STILL-HUNTING

The wet leaves, still glistening with dew, made for quiet footing as the hunter stalked through the second-growth hardwoods. Two careful, deliberate strides, then a halt to scan the surroundings. Then two more strides and a stop. Quiet, minimal movement, watching.

Still-hunters usually prefer a lighter gun—this one was a 6.5-pound 20-gauge Remington 870 pump—since they are virtually always on the move. A compact gun (shorter barrel) is also important, not only to aid moving through brush, but also because it's quicker to point in the up-close-and-personal situations often encountered in dense woodlots.

As with stand hunting, choice of gauge is not critical because the shooting will generally be at close range. One consideration, however, is that the still-hunter may want to use a Foster-style rifled slug. The shorter the projectile in relation to its diameter, the less it is deflected off axis by branches and leaves. The stubby (ballistic coefficient 0.060) rifled slug is thus an ideal short-range brush bucker.

The first hint the stalker had was an antler tip moving slightly in the brush. He brought the gun to his shoulder and focused on the fiber-optic rifle sights just as the bedded buck jumped to its feet and stared, trying to define the intruder he sensed through the intertwined branches between them.

But the brush was simply too thick. The first slug was deflected sufficiently to miss the buck, which quickly took flight. After pumping the action quickly without taking his eyes from the sights, the hunter got a bead on the moving animal and fired again, this time through lighter brush, dropping the 6-pointer cleanly.

Open sights or no-magnification illuminated-dot scopes are excellent choices for both still-hunters and for those who participate in deer drives because they allow the hunter to focus quickly on close-range targets. Still-hunting shotgunners won't be taking longer shots very often in the thick woods most conducive to their chosen hunting method.

DRIVING DEER

Driven animals are usually fleeing in front of the commotion made by the drivers or attempting to sneak out of their way. This doe wasn't sneaking, though. Instead, she was loping through the wood-lot, quartering toward me ahead of the drivers.

Hunting driven animals is another short-range proposition, where the choice of load is pretty much a personal one. The action, though, should be a quick-cycling repeater like a pump or autoloader. My choice on this occasion was a Browning Auto-5 with open sights because it isn't unusual to shoot more than once at animals bounding through saplings. There is no time to pick spots between tree trunks—just blaze away as quickly as possible.

My first two shots tagged small trees, the third put her down for good.

Buckshot is commonly favored over slugs by those who hunt deer driven by dogs, generally in dense understory, because pattern coverage is preferable where brush is apt to deflect individual projectiles.

One of the few times I ever hunted with buckshot, I was on a stand at the edge of a North Carolina swamp. The dogs' howling had gotten progressively louder when, all of a sudden, a buck slipped from his hide 60 yards away and slinked along through the dense underbrush in my direction.

I could see him only intermittently in the snarled vines, but I positioned the big 10-gauge Ithaca Mag-10 autoloader where I thought he was headed. At about 30 yards he stopped, apparently trying to discern the position of the dogs, then bounded off at an angle, quartering toward my position.

The 32-inch barrel swung to an opening in the brush, arriving just as he strode into it. In such short-range situations, optics become more a hindrance than an advantage, but gauge is important. Twelve- and even 10-gauge guns are favored due to the larger pellet count allowed.

As the big gun roared, 12 of the 16 Winchester .34-caliber 00 pellets smashed the buck's chest and shoulder area simultaneously, downing him with a spectacular splash.

The author has taken several bears with shotgun slugs.

OTHER BIG GAME

The vast majority (probably more than 85 percent) of big game hunting with a shotgun is directed at whitetails. But slug guns are often favored by bear hunters shooting over bait (where allowed), and they are the first choice of guides backing up grizzly and brown bear hunters in Alaska.

I've taken black bears, caribou, pronghorns, wild pigs—even a plains bison—with slugs. Not necessarily because slugs were the best choice on each occasion, but rather to demonstrate their effectiveness for a wide range of game animals under the right conditions.

A shotgun loaded with slugs or buckshot is very effective on wild pigs, and, as mentioned, I've taken several with slugs in Texas and California. Twelve- and 10-gauge guns are favored by buckshot users; a high-velocity, flatter-shooting sabot slug is preferred by hunters with rifled barrels. Pigs are very tough and may be en-

This caribou was taken with a Mossberg 500 and Lightfield slugs.

countered at longer ranges, so retained energy and flat trajectory can be important.

Black bears over bait, however, should be taken with big, soft, quick-expansion slugs at short range. The bears I've taken with slugs in Ontario, Manitoba, and Alberta were all shot over bait inside of 50 yards with big-bore slugs like Lightfields and Challengers and an expanding copper sabot, the Remington Copper Solid.

I've taken pronghorns at well over 100 yards in Montana and Wyoming, both with high-velocity sabot slugs. My traveling mate in Wyoming, Steve Meyer, took a bedded buck at an astonishing 191 yards with a Winchester Partition Gold 12-gauge sabot and a Browning A-Bolt slug gun. This isn't something most hunters should try with a shotgun, but it does demonstrate the increasing range of effectiveness of certain loads in expert hands.

The buffalo that fell to my shotgun was an 1,850-pound bull on the same South Dakota ranch where they filmed the movie *Dances with Wolves*. I hit him, walking, in the shoulder at 110 yards with a Winchester Partition Gold and had to finish him with a neck shot at 90 yards. My hunting partner killed a bull with one shot to the neck at 100 yards with the same slug.

I have one friend who handloads slugs for elk hunting and another who took a nice mule deer buck at 165 yards with a slug. Again, a shotgun would never be the first choice for these animals, but their effectiveness was demonstrated on each of the above hunts.

Caribou, on the other hand, are fairly common prey for slug hunters—except in Quebec, where it's illegal to use a shotgun for big game. Despite their size, caribou are fairly frail animals. They are flat-land wanderers with no heavy climbing or sprinting muscles, and I've taken several 400-pound bulls with slugs. In fact, I found shotguns to be the favored ordnance among the native Labrador hunters on my trips to the Far North.

Slug guns are perfectly suited to hunting wild hogs like this one taken on the Nail Ranch in central Texas with a Remington 11–87 and Copper Solid slugs.

Typically, the indigenous hunters used rifled slugs and smoothbores because they were cheaper than rifles and bullets. On the other hand, I used a scoped, rifled-barrel shotgun with sabot slugs because I could. The more sophisticated gun and load came in handy when I shot a bull at 142 yards in a hard crosswind. The scope's crosshairs were placed at nose level about two feet to the left of the animal when I squeezed the trigger, and the wind-deflected slug took him right through the lungs.

While rifles are in little danger of being supplanted by shotguns for most of the above hunting situations, new innovations in shotguns and loads are widening the sphere in which shotguns can be effective hunting tools.

11

TURKEY HUNTING

The big gobbler, who'd been so vocally receptive to my calling when he was out of sight, trundles into view with a Chaplin-like waddle at about 40 yards. Suddenly suspicious when he doesn't see the hen he's been conversing with, the tom drums and begins to strut back and forth, his rope-like beard dragging in the leaves as he does his best to draw the hen into view.

He keeps gobbling, drumming, and strutting, but it soon becomes obvious that he isn't coming any closer unless his perceived mate shows her stuff.

"He's hung up," I whisper to the hunter, Sue. "He's about 40 yards right now, and he'll see us if I move. But he probably won't come any closer without seeing a hen. I didn't have time to set up the decoys because he was coming so fast."

"That's about 10 yards too far for my 20-gauge," says Sue, the disappointment apparent in her voice. "You'd better take him with your 12."

"Oh, all right," I say, trying to sound suitably resigned as greed overcame gallantry and I shouldered my gun.

This scenario once again proved the notion that, at least in the turkey woods and on goose fields, bigger is better—at least ballistically. In a recent magazine article, 20 nationally known turkey hunters were questioned on a variety of topics, one of which was their favored gun and load. Every one selected the biggest possible combination, either 10-gauge or 3½-inch 12-gauge shotguns.

Yes, for ballistic reasons bigger is generally better. But ballistic superiority isn't the only consideration when choosing a shotgun. For instance, I've got an Ithaca Mag-10 with a 32-inch, full-choke barrel that throws a pattern a gnat couldn't slip through at 50 yards. It is absolutely devastating in the winter when geese are tentative and circle rather than drop into the decoys. But in spring turkey season I regularly leave its 12-pound hulk in the gun vault in favor of a 6.5-pound, 12-gauge M37 pump made in the same factory by the same people.

And certainly the denture-rattling 3½-inch 12-gauge isn't everyone's cup of tea, despite the overwhelming firepower. In fact, the first several gobblers I took fell to magnum waterfowl loads (they were lead back then) in a 2¾-inch 12-gauge. To this day, I still favor lighter, faster (and more efficiently patterning) loads to the ultra-

Jeana Sears of Spencer, New York was 10 years old when she took the "grand slam" of North American turkeys with a Remington 1100 Youth Model in 1999.

magnum 12s and 10s. By the same token, the 20-gauge isn't a poor choice for some folks.

Let's start out with the basic premise that any gauge shotgun, with any load, is sufficient to turn out the lights on a turkey, although with smaller gauges the bird must be much closer for the load to be effective. Basically, the larger the gauge the more efficient it is for clean, reliable kills at longer distances.

The trouble is that a 10-gauge autoloader will likely tip the scales in double-digits, with a 12-gauge semi-auto about nine pounds. Single-shots and pumps are lighter, but that is more than offset by the greatly increased mule-kick recoil. Switch to a 20-gauge in any action and you'll probably trim a couple of pounds off the 12 and have a substantially lighter gun than the 10. All of that means a great deal to a smaller shooter or the guy who hikes long distances in the turkey woods. On the other hand, a heavier gun metes out less perceived recoil. It's all a trade-off.

Turkey guns are designed to be aimed like a rifle rather than pointed like a shotgun.

Are you shooting the right gauge for you? Let's find out.

To give people an idea of the difference in gauges, I start off my turkey hunting shotgun seminars with a question: If, God forbid, you ever get hit with a couple of stray No. 6 pellets, would you rather they be fired from a 10-gauge or .410?

Invariably, the audience opts for the perceived weakness of the tiny .410 over the magnum influence of the 10-gauge. But that perception is flawed. A No. 6 pellet, regardless of gauge, is a No. 6 pellet—0.110 inch in diameter. Size and mass being equal, velocity makes the difference in energy and penetration. In actuality, pellets fired from either gun would start out at about 1,200 to 1,250 feet per second, and downrange the .410 might even be traveling slightly faster due to the increased pressures in the small bore. That means the .410 would have as much, if not more, energy and therefore would penetrate farther—and cause more pain—than the cannon-like 10-bore.

Another perception is that bigger bores are more powerful and therefore shoot farther. Wrong again. Identical pellets fired at the same velocity will travel the same distance with the same energy and trajectory. If your 20-gauge will put several pellets in a turkey's head and neck at 40 yards, it's just as effective as a 12- or 10-gauge that prints the same number of pellets there.

But a bigger gauge will give you a bigger pattern; right? Well, yes, but only marginally, and not enough to make a difference. Believe it or not, 20-, 12-, and 10-gauge patterns, given the same choke constriction, will be virtually the same diameter at any given range. That is, if your 12-gauge full-choke pattern is 12 inches wide at 15 yards, a similarly constricted 20-gauge or 10-gauge pattern would theoretically be a foot wide at that distance, also. As noted in the chapter on chokes, however, larger gauges will usually produce a marginally wider pattern since there are more pellets, and therefore more deformation and crowding outward.

Knowing your pattern pays off when that gobbler comes calling.

There is, of course, an obvious ballistic advantage to larger gauges. That's because in a scattergun the energy is a cumulative effect of how many pellets hit the target. There are simply more pellets in a larger gauge hull and therefore more pellets in the pattern—giving the bigger gauge loads more energy.

Using No. 6 shot for comparison since it patterns easily in most any gauge shotgun, you'll find more than 500 pellets in a 2¼-ounce, 10-gauge load compared to 155 in the heaviest .410 load (¹¹⁄₁₆ ounce). For more usable data, consider that there are about 450 pellets in the average 3-inch, 2-ounce, No. 6, 12-gauge turkey load (366 in the high-velocity 1⅝-ounce loads) and 280 in a 20-gauge hull.

You can make whatever gauge gun you're shooting more effective simply by finding a load and a choke constriction that puts the most possible pellets in the center of the pattern—not necessarily the most holes in the paper but rather the most in the head and neck area. I've seen some custom-choked 20s that would outperform virtually all factory-choked 12s at equal ranges.

So maybe with the lesser gauges you will simply have to be a little closer to the bird. But then, what's wrong with that?

CHOOSING THE BEST TURKEY LOAD

"Damn, I really like the sound of this Cop'R Tone slate—too bad the turkeys don't," I was thinking after an extended but fruitless calling session on a tomb-silent Alabama morning last spring.

Just then guide Mike Parrillo, Jr. nudged my arm and quietly pointed out that I had seriously underestimated the birds' appreciation of the new Woods Wise call. A gobbler was just coming out to strut about 40 yards away and was craning his neck to see the harem of hens that must be toward our calling position.

"Long beard," Mike mouthed silently and unnecessarily, apparently to confirm that this bird indeed met the criteria for harvest under the White Oak Plantation's management rules. Striker still in hand, I froze until the gobbler's head moved behind a bush. Then, in what I regarded as a discreet move, I deftly traded the striker for the Ithaca M87 in my lap and brought the latter to battery. The transition was not ignored by some curious hens, though, and a couple of nervous *putts* from them got Mike a little nervous, too.

"Better shoot quick before he makes us too," was his professional advice.

Under normal circumstances I would never take a 40-plus-yard shot with a load of No. 6 shot, but this time I didn't even hesitate. Within a nanosecond of my squeezing the trigger, the 1.5-ounce swarm of Hevi-Shot pellets turned out the lights on the 22-pound gobbler.

Two weeks later, hunting the famed Ford Ranch in Texas, I took two big Rio Grande gobblers at 22 yards and 42 yards. I closed the door on the season in May with a 30-yard shot on an Eastern gobbler in New York. All impressive slam-dunk kills with the same gun and load.

The author was able to take this Alabama bird at 42 yards because he knew how his gun patterned.

I was confident of the results in each case only because, through range testing, I knew the patterning characteristics and other capabilities of that particular load in that particular gun. Choice of load and/or pellet size for your gun is critical, and I'm constantly amazed at how many hunters go afield with a load selected from a suggestion rather than a range session. Making such a crucial decision based on a magazine article, advertising claim, or store clerk's suggestion is silly. No, make that stupid; even unethical.

Chances are that neither the magazine writer nor the store clerk has patterned your gun—so they obviously wouldn't know which load is best for you. You are the only judge.

Consider, first of all, that there is only so much room in a shotgun hull. The more space you take up with pellets the less space there is for propellant. Let's see, heavier payload and less powder. . . . I never took a physics course in school, but I can tell you that this particular equation is definitely not headed toward bigger being better.

Plated and buffered shot patterns 30% better than conventional lead loads.

The big loads are the slowest and least powerful you can select. Oh, they are dynamite killers at 30 to 35 yards with all those extra pellets. But they lose energy very fast, and despite the pellet count, they can be disappointing at the patterning board.

Choke constriction and barrel configuration should dictate what size load and/or pellets your gun will shoot best. Typically, a tighter choke won't like bigger pellets and—if the barrel isn't back-bored—may prefer a smaller payload. Winchester was the first to buck the maximum payload trend in 1997 when it introduced its 1¾-ounce high velocity loads, which earned an immediate reputation for killer patterns. Federal and Remington have since followed suit with small, quick loads.

How about pellet size? There used to be two schools of thought: use small pellets to get numbers in the pattern (there are 225 pellets in an ounce of No. 6 shot but only 135 in an ounce of No. 4s), or use big stuff for better energy retention downrange. Both schools had their merits, but pellet size and count mean nothing if they aren't concentrated in a good pattern.

As a means of gainful employment I spend a great deal of time at the range. Through extensive experimentation, I found that my Ithaca (essentially backbored with lengthened forcing cones at both the chamber and choke) fitted with a 0.660 Rhino choke tube was not overly enamored of 2-ounce loads of copper-plated lead No. 4s or No. 5s, and only tolerated the ultimate load size of No. 6. But the same set-up throws an absolute maelstrom pattern at 30 to 40 yards with Winchester High-Velocity No. 5s—a 1¾-ounce load with 13 percent less pellets in the hull.

Hevi-Shot, however, changed everything. I'd been very impressed with Hevi-Shot as a goose load when it was being loaded by Polywad, and I smiled sagely when Remington announced that it had come to an agreement with EnvironMetal (Hevi-Shot developer) to load and market the tungsten-nickel product as a turkey and waterfowl load.

Remington's experimentation found that the Hevi-Shot, being harder than steel and 10 percent denser than lead, had unique flight and patterning characteristics. Big Green's research showed that a choke constriction of 0.052 in a 12-gauge bore would produce 90-plus-percent patterns at 40 yards. Traditional extra-full turkey chokes (like my Rhino) were too tight.

I proved it to myself by patterning a variety of Hevi-Shot loads. I found that regardless of pellet size, the 1⅞-ounce loads didn't fly well at all out of the 0.660 Rhino and that the tight tube tolerated the 1.5-ounce loads only slightly better.

It's a true luxury to have a custom gun and choke builder as a buddy, and a quick call to Mark Bansner in Adamstown, Pennsylvania got a 0.675 tube sent to my door. The Remington-suggested constriction was perfect, and the gun now throws a Hevi-Shot pattern that a gnat couldn't squeeze through—94 to 96 percent at 40 yards with the Bansner choke installed.

I noted earlier in the waterfowling discussion that while testing Federal's tungsten-iron waterfowl loads I was able to shoot BBs

The shotgun load is your last link to success in turkey hunting.

completely through 20-gauge galvanized sheet metal at 30 yards. Hevi-Shot is much the same. Steel wouldn't penetrate the metal at that range, and lead and bismuth wouldn't penetrate at 15 yards, flattening upon impact instead. That flattening is actually preferred for waterfowl hunting because it means the pellets are expending all of their energy into the body of the bird rather than ripping through.

But turkey loads are designed to smash and penetrate skulls and vertebrae, not make body shots, and tungsten-iron will definitely do that—at long ranges. Federal Cartridge touts its 1,450-fps Premium Tungsten-Iron (comparable in mass to Hevi-Shot) as a 70-yard goose load. The 1,300-fps tungsten-iron turkey load with No. 4 shot should be a killer at 50 to 60 yards if it patterns well in your gun.

Patterning in tight turkey chokes may be a problem, however. The extreme hardness of the shot requires a very thick shotcup to protect the barrel, which accounts for the smaller load (1⅜ ounces).

I found that the tungsten-iron waterfowl loads patterned much like steel—a more open choke was needed to maintain dense patterns, and they weren't always consistent. My guess is that Federal ballisticians lowered the velocity for the turkey load so as to lessen trauma to the shot charge in the barrel and thus improve patterning in more constricted chokes.

In other loads, Remington and Federal offer a wide range of 2¾-, 3-, and 3½-inch 12-gauge; 3½-inch 10-gauge; and 3-inch 20-gauge specialty copper-plated turkey loads, the latter recently adding No. 5 shot to its 10- and 20-gauge selections. Remington also offers an SP Duplex load—a payload of No. 4 and No. 6 pellets in the same hull—in three 12-gauge loadings.

Winchester, in addition to the High Velocity turkey load, also offers a full line of 3½-inch 10- and 12-gauge copper-plated loads, as well as 2¾- and 3-inch 12-gauge loads and a 3-inch 20-gauge.

When Activ went out of business, its nickel-plated Penetrator loads went with it. Kent Cartridge of America, which bought Activ's factory, came out with its own tungsten-matrix turkey load.

Hevi-Shot has stepped right in there as an easy-to-pattern, devastatingly effective turkey load. It didn't show the difficult-to-pattern tendencies shown by other tungsten-alloy loads. And even though Hevi-Shot has 17 less pellets in the hull than a comparable 1⅞-ounce load of copper-plated lead shot, the pattern has a much denser core than any other dispersion I've ever experienced.

Hevi-Shot also throws the shot-size debate out the window. An exhaustive Winchester study in the 1980s showed that No. 6 lead pellets lost their absolute-lethal energy at 32 yards, while No. 4s carried it to nearly 40 yards. Hevi-Shot's density advantage makes No. 6s (which are much easier to pattern out of virtually any gun) lethal at even longer range than lead No. 4s—so you can imagine the potential of No. 4 Hevi-Shot.

But I can't say that Hevi-Shot is the answer in your gun. After all, I've never patterned your gun with various loads. Have you? Getting the most effective load for your gun is, for my money, the most important facet of turkey hunting.

Yes, that's just my opinion. There is, after all, a percentage of the hunting community that will put calling at the head of the class. If you can't entice the bird, they say, it's much more difficult to bag him. Then there are those who see camouflage as the most important element. Concealment is absolutely essential when fooling a bird with very acute, 270-degree, full-color vision.

I'd also have to agree with those who see set-up and woodsmanship as prime factors in successful turkey hunting. But you have to realize that the best caller, wearing the perfect camouflage, set-up in just the right place can still see his or her hunt go sour if the trigger is pulled and the bird flies away.

Is your load up to the challenge?

Your turkey load is like fishing line—the final connection between you and your prey. After everything else is done right, your load, alone, is the determining factor in whether or not you are successful.

DECIDE AT THE PATTERNING RANGE

My suggestion on turkey loads is to narrow down the field through research (friends, books, magazines, store clerks) and take a select variety of loads to the practice range.

Start shooting at a large piece of paper (at least 40 × 40 inches) at 15 yards. Shoot from a bench if possible and aim at a dot in the center, using any load. This exercise tells you where the gun shoots in relation to point of aim. Many guns shoot slightly off-center, and some shoot a lot off-center. If your gun doesn't center the pattern exactly where you put the bead you might consider using adjustable sights or a scope that can be adjusted to compensate.

The patterning board is the only place to find the optimum load for your gun.

Once that has been established, move back to 25 yards and shoot each load from the bench or rested position at large sheets of paper. Remember that patterning a turkey gun is much different than patterning a gun for wingshooting. Turkey hunters don't necessarily need a nice, round, clean pattern with the shot evenly dispersed. They want a tight pattern that can be ragged at the edges. But it must have a very dense core that can be centered on a standing bird's head and neck. You aim a turkey gun like a rifle, not like a shotgun. Sights, particularly rifle-like sights, are a distraction to wingshooters but a godsend to turkey hunters for this very reason.

A few shots at 25 yards will tell you which load patterns most cleanly from your particular barrel. Remember, you're not looking for the best pellet dispersion but rather for a dense core in the pattern.

When the best patterning loads are determined, walk away from the bench and switch patterns. Using turkey head patterns, which are available from a variety of manufacturers, shoot at a clean target at a variety of ranges. Using a sitting position like you would in the woods, shoot first at 10 yards, then 15, 20, 25, 30, 35, and 40.

The first shots of your patterning session should come from a bench.

After determining whether your shotgun shoots straight, move to a natural shooting position to start patterning at various ranges.

Note how the pattern changes with yardage. Does it remain dense? How many pellets are striking the head and neck area? At what yardage does the best pattern begin to deteriorate?

And remember, regardless of gauge, similarly choked guns (compare full choke to full choke, extra-full to extra-full) will throw the same dimension and size pattern. The only difference will be the number of pellets in the pattern, since larger bores throw heavier shot charges.

This simple exercise will not only tell you which load is best for your gun, it will also tell you the size of your pattern at specific ranges—a real advantage if a bird steps into a small opening 40 yards away or surprises you by popping up at 12 yards.

FACTORING IN RECOIL

I was guiding a student through a patterning session at the turkey hunting school at Turkey Trot Acres hunting lodge in Candor, New

York. Getting ready for his first-ever turkey season, the 35-year-old student from New Jersey was intent on centering his first shot on the patterning board at 30 yards, squeezing his 12-gauge, 3.5-inch Mossberg 835 pump tight to his shoulder.

"Line up both beads with the bull's-eye and exhale slowly while squeezing the trigger, Ron," I coached in his ear at the shooting bench.

Boom!

Ron lurched violently backward and moaned while pumping the gun open to eject the empty hull.

"Okay, that one was pretty much centered," I said, looking at the patterning board. "Let's put up more paper and shoot a couple more times to get a good pellet count."

"Forget it!" said Ron, rubbing his shoulder. "We're going to have to go with what we've got off the first target. I'm not shooting that thing again until it's absolutely necessary. The guy at the store told me the 3½ inch is the most powerful turkey gun you can get. After this I'm not so sure I need that much power just to kill a bird."

There is obviously a price to pay for the ultimate big-bore turkey guns. The 3½-inch 12- and 10-gauge guns are definitely devastating on targets, but they also hit hard on the other end.

The big Mossberg 835 was the first 12-gauge pump shotgun ever chambered for 3½-inch shells. Browning's BPS followed, then Remington's 870 and Benelli's Nova.

RULE OF NINETY-SIX

British gunbuilder William Wellington Greener was not only an innovative designer but also a respected researcher and author. His 1881 work *The Gun and Its Development* is a classic that is still used as a reference book today. The book introduced a standard that is known as "Greener's Rule of Ninety-Six." Simply stated, Greener's calculations showed that a shotgun should be 96 times heavier than the weight of the shot charge it fires in order to ensure good patterns, the shooter's comfort, and the longevity of the firearm.

Applying this rule, a shotgun firing 1 ounce of shot should weigh 6 pounds. A load of 1⅛ ounces is better suited for a 6¾-pound gun; 7½-pound guns are needed to handle 1¼-ounce loads. Of the many pronouncements made by early gunmakers, this one is generally accepted as gospel—meaning today's loads are way out of whack.

"What do you expect?" said one outspoken expert in the shotgun ammunition field. "You're shoving what is essentially an 8-gauge load down a 12-gauge barrel. That's a lot of pressure that has to go somewhere."

Recoil is definitely a consideration with the ultimate big-bore turkey guns.

Consider that the average 2-ounce, 3-inch 12-gauge load—the most popular turkey load sold—shoves the butt of a 7-pound pump-gun into your shoulder at 19.265 feet per second for a measured recoil of 43 foot-pounds. Most of you will be able to confirm these figures with experience; 3-inch turkey loads certainly get your attention at ignition. By comparison, the Barnes Ballistic Program shows that the renowned hard-kicking .375 H&H magnum rifle loaded with its optimum 270-grain hunting load only develops 39.5 foot-pounds of recoil.

Now let's consider the big boys. The 3½-inch turkey load in the 7-pound, 12-ounce Mossberg 835 pump develops a whopping 60.3 foot-pounds of recoil, hitting your shoulder at a speed of 22.31 feet per second. For comparison, that's 6 foot-pounds more than a .416 Remington Magnum with a 700-grain bullet—the gun's suggested load for elephants!

The 10-gauge, given its roomier bore and hull and greater gun heft but identical-size load, is far less punishing, despite a 60 fps velocity advantage over the stoked-to-the-limit 3½-inch 12 gauge. A 2¼-ounce 10-gauge load fired from my 11-pound Ithaca Mag-10 develops

Reading a turkey gun's signature.

48.7 foot-pounds of recoil at a speed of 16.88 feet per second. That's no love tap, but it is considerably less formidable than the long 12.

So is the 10-gauge and its 3½-inch 12-gauge stepbrother too much gun for turkeys? Or is the real question whether they are too much for turkey hunters?

The 2¼-ounce payload is ¼ ounce larger than the conventional 3-inch 12-gauge shell capacity. That means 34 more No. 4 pellets (or 42 more No. 5s or 50 more No. 6s) in the longer hull. But with a federally mandated chamber pressure ceiling of 12,500 feet per square inch on all loads, the bigger hull can't add sufficient powder to drive the payload any faster than its smaller brethren. In fact, in most cases the 2¼-ounce load is slightly slower than the 2-ouncer. Thus, the ballistic advantage the 2¼-ounce load holds over conventional 3-inchers is marginal. And the cost is extremely excessive recoil.

The most popular and commonly available 10-gauge guns today are the Remington SP-10 autoloader (an updated Ithaca Mag-10 design) and Browning Gold autoloader and the Browning BPS-

10 pump. NEF's single-shot 10-gauge Turkey Special weighs almost 10 pounds. The autoloaders weigh 11 pounds apiece and incorporate gas-operated recoil systems.

The 3½-inch chambered Mossberg 835 Ultri-Mag weighs 7 pounds, 12 ounces and quakes mightily when that "8-gauge load" is forced down the barrel. The 9-pound Browning BPS is only marginally gentler when handling the 3½-inch loads.

When all the information is weighed and tallied the figures show that, yes, the 2¼-ounce payloads from 3½-inch 12- and 10-gauge guns are indeed the biggest, baddest loads available for turkey hunting. You just have to ask yourself if the marginally better performance is worth the hit you'll take every time you pull the trigger. Not to mention the possibility of developing a flinch in anticipation of what is to come. . . .

COSMETIC SURGERY FOR YOUR SHOTGUN

How many of us wish we'd had the opportunity—or the money—to purchase a fully camouflaged version of a turkey or waterfowl gun? Or maybe you are stuck with a favorite gun that simply wasn't available with a camo option, at least not one in your favorite pattern.

Well, there is a solution—besides covering the gun with the camouflage tape of the moment, or hand-painting using small leaves as templates. It's called Second Skin, a process that can apply the camouflage coating of your choice to your current shotgun using the same method that is commercially applied on new specialty rifles, shotguns, muzzleloaders, and bows.

The price (about $150) is comparable to a re-blueing or stock refinishing job. The pattern also protects the coated pieces from corrosion. On used guns the parts are thoroughly degreased, then painted with a base coat and primer coat. When both have

Second Skin can perform cosmetic surgery on your shotgun.

been dried and taped, a sheet of film is placed on the surface of an immersion tank filled with water heated to a specific temperature. The film, which holds the camouflage pattern, is then sprayed with an activator that dissolves the film, leaving the colors in the water. The part is dipped into the colors, which adhere to the surface. It is then rinsed, dried, inspected, and sent to a touch-up room.

The high-quality results are definitely worth the money for serious turkey hunters—and waterfowlers, for that matter.

12

![line]

SHOOTING GAMES

SPORTING CLAYS

Chances are your great-grandfather was a pretty fair wingshot. Back then a man could learn to shoot in the field. Bag limits were generous or unheard-of and game was plentiful. If he missed or made a mistake—prime elements of the learning process—it was not critically important.

But today the game is different. Small bag limits, time constraints, more hunter competition on less ground, and a general lack of game makes it virtually impossible for the average gunner to improve, let alone perfect, his shotgunning technique in true hunting situations. And it was this notion that spawned claybird shooting. It all started as a means of practicing the most difficult aspect of hunting—wingshooting for upland birds and waterfowl.

Magazines, celebrities, and noted writers have picked up the game of sporting clays in the last decade and run with it, giving it more exposure than Madonna's cleavage. Clubs have carved courses out of wooded acreage, added a few simple traps, and *voila!*—a sporting clays course. Operating on the Kevin Costner–inspired belief that "if you build it, they will come," club after club has

Sporting clays is a game that combines various aspects of trap, skeet, hunting, and even golf.

found that a decent sporting clays layout outranks any chicken dinner or gun raffle as a steady revenue producer.

Formal sporting clays competition didn't reach America until the 1980s, but the game wasn't a totally foreign concept. Clubs and preserves have had special claybird set-ups for decades. I've encountered more than a few "crazy quail" courses with a couple of traps situated to duplicate the tougher angles taken by bobwhites. The Campfire Club of New York has for decades maintained a Hunters Clays course, begun after a member's introduction to the sport on a visit to England.

It's easy enough to trace the development of the modern claybird. American George Ligowsky's 1880s idea of saucers composed of baked river silt and pitch became logical successors to glass balls and virtually spelled the end of live bird shoots. An Englishman named McCaskey improved on Ligowsky's idea by substituting limestone for river silt—the recipe for today's birds—and the first U.S. clay target trapshoot took place in 1885 at New Orleans, Louisiana.

In the 1920s New Englander Charles Davies, dissatisfied with trap's lack of crossover and incoming shots, set out to develop a game that offered more shots encountered while hunting. Skeet was thus born. But trap and skeet shooters couldn't get realistic practice at shooting incoming doves, flushing pheasants, springing teal, overhead mallards, straight-away geese, bounding rabbits, and passing quail.

It was about the same time in England that a shooting game was devised that incorporated shots from both skeet and trap. Sporting, as the game was called, was established by some of Britain's top gunmakers on their private hunting grounds. Sporting clays was a derivative of that game and has since become the most popular shooting game in the British Isles.

We do know that Remington Arms involved the National Rifle Association and the National Shooting Sports Foundation in the introduction of Hunters Clays to North America in the 1960s. Remington commissioned Briton Chris Craddock to design a course at Remington Farms in Maryland.

The whole idea was to introduce a shooting game that offered far less predictable targets than trap and skeet and one where champions didn't need Mercedes-priced specialty guns and garb and where titles weren't constantly a matter of multi-gun shoot-offs among perfect scorers. It was to be a game for which the average upland hunter could use his field gun and get useful practice along with a challenge and some entertainment.

Sporting clays has been described as a combination of skeet, trap, and golf. The game incorporates the hard-crossing target angles of skeet, the rising straight-aways of trap—and several other targets. It is contested, like golf, on stations strewn over the countryside. Each station typically incorporates aspects of the terrain with unique target angles. There may be 10 to 20 stations, depending on the course. Some are 50-bird layouts, others 100.

Clays courses adapt their shooting stations to the existing terrain.

The targets are listed at each station, commonly two singles and a report, or true pair. The first shooter in a group commonly asks to see the birds thrown before he or she gets into position to shoot. When the "sighters" have been observed, the shooter stands ready (gun already mounted in casual shoots, low-gun position required at registered shoots) and calls for the bird or birds. Each competitor shoots his or her sequence before the next shooter takes the position.

While skeet and trap call for muscle memory, sporting clays—like field hunting—rewards proper body mechanics and flexibility on the muzzle swing. Proper foot placement and fluidity in the hips and torso are critical, and a huge emphasis is placed on smooth, spontaneous reaction.

Remington's introduction proved to be a bit premature as the real interest in sporting clays didn't develop in a major way until world-renowned gun writer Bob Brister of Texas got his first taste of

In sporting clays, the shooter gets a different type of shot at each station.

the game on a trip to England in the early 1980s. His coverage of his experience persuaded Orvis to incorporate the game into its shooting schools and everything started to snowball. True, you're apt to pay as much as 10 times more for a round of sporting clays than you do for same amount of trap or skeet targets. But it's fun, challenging, and damned good practice for the field.

The first organized sporting clays tournament on record was in 1983 in Brister's Houston. In 1985 the now-defunct United States Sporting Clays Association was formed by a small group of influential Houston shooters, and the world heard about it at the Shooting, Hunting, and Outdoor Trade (SHOT) Show in 1986. In 1989 a second organization, the National Sporting Clays Association, was formed as an offshoot of the National Skeet Shooting Association in San Antonio, Texas. The NSCA is recognized as the sport's sanctioning body in North America today.

WHAT YOU NEED FOR SPORTING CLAYS

If you do any bird hunting, chances are you already have what you'll need to get started with sporting clays. Unlike trap and skeet shooting, where field equipment puts you at a distinct disadvantage to the specialized ordnance and garb of the experienced competitors, sporting clays is a hunter's game.

For most people, a 12-gauge field gun with open chokes is fine. (Ten-gauges aren't usually allowed on sporting clays courses.) For ammunition, shot sizes from No. 7½ to 9 are common and effective. An upland bird vest or jacket will serve you just as well on the sporting clays course as a special skeet or trapshooting coat—you're only looking for a little shoulder padding and a surface on which the gun-butt won't slip.

Adequate ear and eye protection are also necessities, but only the irresponsible go to the range without them in this day and age. And it probably wouldn't hurt to accessorize a bit by purchasing a shell bag. Other than adequate disposable income, there is little else needed to get started.

If your interest in sporting clays increases, of course, fine-tuning those "necessities" may be worthwhile. Let's take a closer look at the various elements.

Shotgun

I started shooting clays with a battle-scarred Browning Auto-5 because that's what I had hunted birds with for decades. The hump-backed autoloader was fine and worked well for me since I was only shooting to practice for hunting. That was fine until I shot a round with a borrowed over-under.

The over-under is the most prevalent sporting clays gun today for the same reasons that it is so popular as a bird gun: it's light, well-balanced, quick to point, and easy to swing while carrying all the ammunition you'll need. There are plenty of national-class clays

Foot-operated traps allow a shooter to practice wingshooting alone.

shooters, however, who shoot Remington, Benelli, and Beretta autoloaders.

My current clays gun is an Ithaca/Fabarms Gamma with 26-inch barrels. That's a tad short for the avid shooter because it takes a more concerted effort to swing the barrels. I make the most of it because it's also a constant grouse hunting companion and a true joy in the dove fields. But most experienced sporting clays shooters today want 30-, 32-, or even 34-inch barrels.

The recoil pad on a sporting clays gun should have a rounded top so that it doesn't snag the shirtsleeve or vest of the shooter as it is mounted from the low-gun position after the target is called for.

Loads

Anything over a 1-ounce load is too much on a sporting clays course, and manufacturers are producing special ⅞- and 1-ounce sporting clays and "international" loads. Inexpensive game loads available from mass merchandisers are every bit as effective as the expensive specialty loads. They simply kick harder and pattern a few percentage points lower than the top-shelf stuff.

I've found that Federal's ⅞-ounce International load patterns extremely well and shoots gently in my gun. But I've also found that Wal-Mart's pricing on game loads often drops to within 40 cents of the cost I incur when reloading a box, making it an inexpensive substitute.

As mentioned earlier, anything from No. 7½ to 9 shot is adequate, but as you improve and get experience with various shots, you'll find that the bigger pellets are more effective on the hard clay "rabbits" and at stations where the bird is thrown in profile, offering only a view of its rim as it flies flat. Elsewhere, No. 8, 8½, and 9 shot are preferred due to the superior number of pellets they provide in the pattern.

As much as I hate to see it, there are serious sporting clays shooters today who have specific handloads for specific stations. They're looking for trap-load performance at the long rising shots, skeet-load characteristics for minis and closer targets.

Chokes

I use skeet and improved cylinder chokes for all courses and seldom feel undergunned. I have seen some shooters who swear by modified chokes and have even seen a course or two where that might be the preferred constriction, given the extreme distance of the targets. Just remember that this is still claybird shooting, and you only need a couple of pellets to score—so get as many pellets in the flight zone as possible.

It is very important, however, to test-shoot a variety of load and pellet sizes through your choke system. Some will pattern very well and others pitifully; there's no way to predict performance since they all react differently to different guns.

Five-stand is a variation of sporting clays that is shot on a small course.

Protection

Eye and ear protection are no-brainers. Shooting glasses, whether the fashionable wrap-around variety or the functional pilot's style, should feature a shatter-resistant lens tinted a color that doesn't hide neon-orange clays (as some do). As for ear protection, conventional foam inserts have been shown to be adequate. Muffs are more effective and very popular, but some shooters have problems mounting the gun without interference from the domed earpiece.

There are several sophisticated hearing protection devices on the market, also. Since I wear a cowboy hat, muffs are out. I also lost a lot of my hearing from shooting before I was smart enough to wear protection. The answer for me is the Target Ear, a hearing-aid type unit that loops over one ear (the other is plugged with a foam pad). The Target Ear allows me to hear range commands, the trap release, and casual conversation but blocks any sounds over 90 decibels (my 12-gauge's bark is 130 decibels), well within accepted limits for hearing health.

SHOOTERS ARE ATHLETES

Good shooting requires good eye-hand coordination, flexibility, and muscle tone.

I had an opportunity to spend some time with world-class shooters when I worked as a press liaison at the Wolf Creek Shooting Venue for the 1996 Olympic Games in Atlanta, and I was impressed with their attention to what and when they ate and drank and how much they rested.

Food, stress, and physical activity all have an effect on your breathing rate and pulse—two key factors in accurate shooting. The old suggestion of taking a deep breath and exhaling a little

Olympic shooters are world-class athletes in terms of physical talent and preparation.

while you press the trigger is relatively easy to accomplish. Controlling your heart rate is more difficult. Heart rate is lowest in the early morning, before you eat. Research by shooters has shown that eating even simple foods, such as a banana, will increase heart rate at least 10 beats per minute. Coffee or a sugary carbonated drink will often cause an increase of as much as 50 beats per minute.

Sugar, caffeine, and carbon dioxide are virtually equal in their influence on heart rate. Tobacco, the excessive use of salt, stimulants, alcohol, and refined white flour have cumulative corrosive effects on blood vessels, causing them to stiffen, which causes the heart to pump faster to deliver sufficient oxygen to the system.

A good daily multi-vitamin combined with extra amounts of vitamins C (6 to 8 grains per day), A, B, and D, and at least 2,000 international units of E may help improve eyesight and mental clarity to the point that shooting scores will improve.

SKEET SHOOTING

It's a little known fact that complaints from a neighbor in 1926 changed skeet shooting to the format that it follows today. Charles Davies of Andover, Massachusetts is credited with devising the original game of "Shooting Around the Clock," in which one trap was used and shooters moved around it in a circle. When a neighbor complained about the direction of the shooting, Davies cut the circle in half and added a second trap opposite the first, which he eventually raised to add variety.

National Sportsman magazine promoted the game, but it lacked a good name and the magazine ran a contest to come up with one. The $100 first prize went to a woman who submitted the name "skeet," which is a Scandinavian word for "shoot."

Skeet is a popular game of hard-crossing targets in which the sustained-lead method of shooting can be used.

An American skeet field has eight shooting positions, seven of which are arranged in a half-circle facing the line between the two traps. The eighth is directly between the traps. The left-hand house is elevated much higher than the right. At each station contestants shoot one target from each house. On stations No. 1, 2, 6, and 7 they also shoot at targets released simultaneously from the two houses. Twenty-five targets make up a round. Unlike trapshooting, which is essentially a 12-gauge game, skeet is contested in 12-, 20-, 28-, and .410-gauges.

TRAPSHOOTING

How did trapshooting get its name? The game, which originated in England, started with live pigeons as targets. The pigeons were trapped under top hats and flew when the hats were tipped by a string operated by the "puller." As the game evolved, box traps replaced the top hats and glass balls filled with feathers or soot replaced the pigeons. Eventually, brightly colored, easy-to-throw clay disks became the targets.

Trapshooters use moderate to tightly choked 12-gauge guns with raised barrel ribs to make them shoot high, since the targets are rising. All of the targets are going away from the shooter at a longer distance and tighter angle than most skeet or sporting clays targets.

Five shooting positions are aligned parallel 16 yards behind the game's single trap position. The traphead moves constantly side-to-side, releasing birds at random angles on the shooter's command. Each shooter fires a single shot in rotation until five shots have been achieved, at which time the contestants move to the next station.

The handicap version of the game is the same as 16-yard trap except that the contestants stand at varying distances from the trap house, based on their ability, as determined by previous scores. Handicap stances range from 20 to 27 yards. There is also a game of doubles that is contested at 16 yards, in which two targets fly simultaneously.

13

KEEPING IT CLEAN

Cleaning a gun after a day of shooting is like washing dishes after a great meal. It's a necessary chore—payment for the enjoyment previously received. While everyone knows that guns should be cleaned regularly, it is probably the most neglected aspect of shooting.

BARRELS

Heavy fouling has undoubtedly retired more guns than worn barrels. Nothing destroys a gun's pattern or groups faster or ruins a barrel sooner than fouling. Fresh fouling may look fairly innocent when viewed in the bore. After all, the advent of shotcups has all but eliminated lead fouling. But you should realize that powder, primer, and plastic wad residue gets ironed into the barrel walls of the bore every time a load passes through. This fouling attracts moisture and traps it against the barrel walls. What follows with time obviously isn't good for your gun.

In shotguns, a pattern suddenly going awry isn't the worst thing that can happen. Powder and plastic wad fouling reach a point where they drag on subsequent shotcups and pull them away from loads, thus negating their controlling, containing function.

Cleaning your shotgun after a day afield isn't much fun, but it is vitally important for accuracy and longevity.

Outdoor writers often act like experts in all fields, but that's only because they know what experts to contact to make them look good. In my case, when looking for shooting information, I go to folks obsessed with firearms performance—benchrest shooters and registered trap or skeet shooters. These guys are the test pilots of the shooting industry. Their research, testing, tinkering, and application has contributed much to the general sport of shooting.

One of the main contributions from these experts is the notion that a sanitary bore and the proper techniques to achieve it are absolute necessities. In a sport where a 5-shot 100-yard group that can't be covered with a dime sends the competitor into apoplexy or where chipping the 100th bird gives a shotgunner pause, precision is a hallmark. It only follows that absolutely clean barrels are a prerequisite.

The same reasoning applies to all firearms, of course—accumulated carbon, copper, lead, and plastic shotgun wad fouling changes tolerances and affects accuracy. Like a race car, no gun can achieve its true potential without a clear track to run on.

When Nitrobenzene was eliminated from bore cleaners (a move we should all applaud for health and environmental reasons), benchrest shooters began to experiment.

"When they outlawed Nitro guys were scrambling. They were trying everything from home brews to blackpowder solvent, spray engine cleaner, even jewelers abrasive," said veteran benchrest competitor and Grand American fixture Sal Ventimiglia of Chagrin Falls, Ohio.

Some early solvents were so strong they would pit or gall stainless steel barrels. Others took hours to work. Ventimiglia's personal "home brew" solvent was so effective and efficient that it gained widespread acceptance among fellow shooters. So widespread, in fact, that it was the basis for the Shooter's Choice line of gun-care products, marketed today by Sal's sons, Joe and Frank.

A wooden dowel and a wrapping of paper towels make a good shotgun cleaning system.

In talking with Ventimiglia and the late Frank Little, possibly trapshooting's all-time most popular and successful figure, I was able to glean a few tips on bore cleaning. First, stay away from hardened steel jointed rods. Jointed aluminum rods are similarly unhealthy. A soft metal like aluminum can pick up grit and act just like a lap, scratching the lands and grooves of a rifled barrel or the mirror finish of a shotgun tube with every stroke.

For shotguns, an excellent patch rod can be made from a ⅝-inch wooden dowel with a bicycle handlebar grip fastened to one end. An absorbent paper towel (I've found Bounty brand works best) folded and rolled to bore-filling diameter is an excellent shotgun cleaning patch. Soak the towel with a quality bore cleaner and push it the length of the bore from chamber to muzzle. Wet brush and wet patch until clean.

Use only phosphorus bronze brushes wound on a core for shotguns or rifles. Stainless steel brushes are so hard they will score some

A well-used shotgun should be cleaned regularly with a special chamber brush.

barrel steel, even chrome liners. I generally run a couple of solvent-soaked patches through the bore and let them sit a few minutes, then hit it with the brush. Wipe out the debris with dry patches until the cloth is clean, then run soaked patches and the brush again. Repeat the process until the dry patches or paper towels come out clean.

Always use a rest, or even a vise with protective pads, to hold the firearm steady while the cleaning rod is worked through the bore. The muzzle should be situated lower than the receiver so that solvents drain away from the chamber and stock wood.

If you are going to shoot the gun again soon, the barrel can be left dry. But I try to leave a thin film of bore solvent in the barrel when I'm finished cleaning to protect it while stored—regardless of how long it will be idle. I like to run a dry patch at the range or in the field before shooting.

BACKBORED BARRELS

Several friends of mine found that they were having problems getting their 12-gauge barrels clean with conventional brushes and rods, no matter how much they tried. In each case the shooter had a backbored barrel that was used for waterfowling or turkey hunting.

Backboring, or over-boring, means that the interior diameter of the barrel is increased to lessen recoil and clean up patterns. For my friends, it also meant that the interior of their 12-gauge barrels actually approached 10-gauge dimensions. As soon as they switched to 10-gauge wound phosphorus bronze brushes and oversize patches the barrels cleaned up just fine.

CHOKE TUBES

Screw-in choke tubes also require special attention. I give my barrels a quick field cleaning after every shooting session. About once a month (every 400 to 500 rounds) I remove the tubes and soak the

Cleaning choke tubes is critical for good performance.

entire barrel in a stainless steel tray filled with bore solvent, then I soak the tubes separately and use a choke-tube brush to cut the plastic deposits that tend to build up in the constriction.

I realize that a couple of gallons of bore solvent is a pretty dear investment. An affordable and suitable alternative can be made by mixing equal parts of kerosene, paint thinner, Dextron III automatic transmission fluid, and Acetone.

CLEANING OTHER PARTS OF YOUR SHOTGUN

I use a special chamber brush to clean the chamber area, which is prone to carbon build-up. Above, I mentioned a quick field cleaning after each shooting session. Competitive trap and skeet shooters will often run a dry patch to catch loose fouling, then a wet patch, leaving the bore in that state for storage. Residue is lifted and suspended in the solvent, which also displaces moisture until the next time you shoot. A dry patch, at least, will be needed before the next time the gun is shot.

Remember that rods should always be wiped clean and brushes should have solvent rinsed out of them. Solvent is meant to dissolve gilded metal and doesn't know the difference between residue and bronze or brass bristles. Clean brushes with a degreasing agent.

Use a toothbrush to scrub bearing surfaces with bore solvent and to clean actions. Then wipe the solvent off, spray with a degreaser, and coat the metal surfaces (including the inside of the tube) with a quality moisture displacer.

When using a grease or oil lubricant the rule of thumb is "if you can see it, it's too much." Use sparingly and always check the temperature range on the product label. If the range isn't listed, chances are you're holding something that turns into gunk in extremely cold weather.

There are plenty of gun-cleaning kits on the market, but the components are just as easy to find at a decent sporting goods store. You'll need appropriately sized cleaning patches, a good rod (Dewey and Bore Tech are excellent, or make your own), and a

Shooter's Choice has an entire line of gun-care products.

bronze brush and bore solvent at the very least. I also like to use a specialty "crudbuster" T-handled choke tube brush and a longer chamber brush for more thorough cleaning. The gun grease or oil is used sparingly and a container of either will last a long time. I also keep an aerosol degreaser handy to spray into just-cleaned actions.

In shotgunning, if you're concerned with patterning or durability or future convenience, the bottom line is that a little tender loving care never hurt any relationship.

WORKING AROUND LEAD

Lead poisoning can be dangerous and debilitating. People who are extremely sensitive to lead should wear a dust mask and rubber gloves when cleaning a firearm.

"Everyone should wash their hands thoroughly with soap and warm water after cleaning a firearm," says gun-care expert Joe Ventimiglia. "The bolt and receiver area are typically loaded with very fine lead particles that can get into your lungs and stomach if you eat immediately without washing the residue from your hands.

"People who shoot at indoor ranges should also be extremely careful. Lead is present in vapor form after each discharge. It is also present in most priming mixtures and in particle form as it shears off from pressure on the driving sides of the rifling lands."

UNBURNT POWDER—THE CURSE OF STEEL SHOT

In terms of ballistics, steel shot is significantly different than lead. For one thing, steel is much harder and lighter. Hunters must change shooting techniques and shot sizes to adjust. They must also clean their guns more often.

Due to some complex internal ballistics characteristics, steel shot uses a slower-burning powder than lead and slower powder means more residue left in the barrel. The powder residue traps plastic wad residue and other foreign particles, which attract moisture and hold it against the walls of the barrel. The fouling not only messes up your pattern, but it can also rust the tube.

Immediately after coming in from the field—especially on those dark, damp days that waterfowl hunting is known for—your gun's chamber and barrel should be worked with a wire brush and bore cleaner.

STORING YOUR GUNS

Back in my youth, when irresponsibility and carelessness were noticeable facets of my character, I screwed up the blueing on a few guns—not all of them mine—by "riding them hard and hanging them up wet," as the saying goes. All it would have taken to avoid the rusting (and the subsequent re-blueing bill for Dad's gun) was a dose of common sense. But that was absent at the time and I learned a lesson the hard way.

After use in rough weather, all guns should obviously be wiped down thoroughly with a dry cloth, disassembled to get at ambient moisture in the interior, and then sprayed liberally with a moisture-displacing agent such as Shooter's Choice Rust Prevent. Apply one coat, let it set for 30 seconds and wipe it off. Then spray again with a lighter coat before putting the gun away in its case or vault for storage. I keep fresh silica bags in my gun vaults at all times to discourage rusting and keep a vigilant eye on the moisture-monitoring strips to better know when to replace the bags.

Common sense dictates that all guns should be stored in a manner that discourages access by unwanted hands. The choice of a storage container depends largely on the owner's concerns and the value of the guns. Certainly a build-the-house-around-it, thick-walled, 100-percent fireproof, bank-certified locking system gun vault fits everyone's needs. But it's overkill for some and prohibitive for most of the rest of us.

In my own case, I own a lot of guns and usually have several others in my shop on loan from manufacturers for testing purposes.

The author uses a Sentry 14 gun safe for storing shotguns.

But I don't own or possess any truly valuable (four-figure price tag) guns, and my shop has fire-resistant ⅝-inch sheetrock walls and a deadbolt door lock. The guns are reasonably protected against fire and outside elements and casual intruders. The main concern for me is keeping folks who do gain entrance to the shop from handling the guns without permission.

Thus, two inexpensive keyed steel gun cabinets bolted to the floor and wall are all I need. In my upstairs gunroom and office, however, which is more accessible and less resistant to fire, I have a Sentry 14 gun safe. It features much thicker walls and a five-deadbolt lock-up to discourage anyone short of a torch-wielding professional.

Again, the guns I have aren't spectacularly valuable, so a $3,000 half-ton fireproof vault isn't necessary. The $600, 375-pound Sentry safe with a wheeled combination lock provides all the security I need.

14

RELOADING FOR SHOTGUNNERS

How much do you really know about how your shotgun works? Outside of the fact that it has more moving parts than Janet Jackson, and makes a loud noise when you trip the trigger, it's probably pretty much a mystery.

I'm one of those guys who can't live that way. I've got to see how things work, and guns have always fascinated me in that regard. Every time a gun comes into the shop I have to take it apart to see what makes it tick. That's also why I reload. When my shotgun goes *Bang!* I have the satisfaction of knowing how and why.

By personally handling all of the components that make up a given load, a shooter is more in touch with the requirements of the shooting conditions. Just taking a box of shells off a dealer's shelf keeps pellet sizes, powder charges, and their applications abstract. Studying the various sizes and parts of a shotshell and considering the conditions under which they will be used connects the shooter with all of the elements of the sport.

That's another reason I got into reloading—the desire to plan, handle, and assemble each load and the subsequent sense of pride

Hull, shot, primers, and powder—all basic components for a shotgun reloader.

and accomplishment when that load performs well. It's the same reason a woman knits a sweater or crafts a quilt when good quality commercial variations are available; the same reason people build their own cabins or boats rather than contracting to have it done. It's the same reason, come to think of it, that I hunt rather than accept my meat butchered and served up in Styrofoam and Cellophane.

Another of the many reasons to handload shotshells is, of course, economy. A reloader can expect to save approximately half the cost of factory shells, usually with superior components. The next most popular reason, I'd guess, would be the ability to tailor a load to your own wants and needs. Customizing ammunition to reduce velocity levels for lower recoil or to adjust shot size and charge weights for specific purpose and performance are advantages for the reloader.

Elsewhere in this book I've written about my 80-year-old, 6½-pound Ithaca 16-gauge side-by-side. It's a carrying gun, meant to travel easily and swing with grace; a light field piece that wasn't designed to handle magnum loads. The chamber even had to be lengthened before it would accept modern ammunition. And try finding a quality light commercial load for a 16-gauge gun these days.

I have a couple of recipes for ingeniously tailored loads with plenty of pop on upland birds and on the clay target range that won't shake my frail little gun apart. The components for those loads are a little more expensive, but they are worth it to me for the enjoyment I get out of shooting that gun.

If you're reloading just for plinking or sporting clays, you can get away with drop (soft) shot; if you're hand loading premium target loads you want more expensive chilled (harder) or plated shot, or even non-toxic alternatives such as steel, bismuth, or tungsten alloys.

Unlike metallic cartridge reloading, each shotshell load carries with it specific and absolute components that must be used. If you can get a good buy on Brand A wads as opposed to the specified Brand B, you can't use them unless you find a load specifying Brand A—regardless of what the well-meaning but under-informed sales-clerk says about interchangeability of components. If you are bargain hunting, take along a reloading manual to determine if data exists for the components you want to buy.

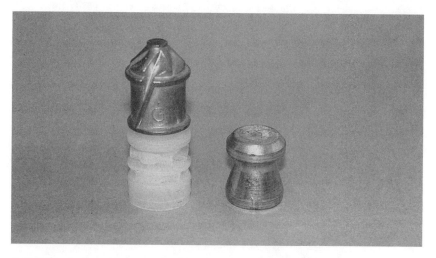

Ballistic Products and Lyman make slugs that can be handloaded.

Savings can also be realized by reusing fired hulls. Typically, the better one-piece hulls can be reloaded about six times. Others, particularly those that use a separate base wad and plastic tube to form the case, are suitable for only one or two reloadings. There are two sources of no-problem cases for the novice: those obtained as the result of firing factory ammunition and those purchased as new components. Good luck trying to find the latter since many manufacturers don't sell their new hulls as components, and not many stores carry them anyway.

I was fortunate to virtually fill the 6-foot bed of my pickup with one-fired Remington Premier hulls on a visit to the Ilion (NY) Rod & Gun Club for the Remington Shooting School some years back. The club is just three miles up the hill from the century-old Remington manufacturing plant, and high-grade Remington loads are all that are used at the schools.

Your biggest cash outlay will be the purchase of reloading equipment, but that cost can be amortized over years of shooting. If you just want to try shotshell reloading to see if you like it, many metallic cartridge reloading presses can be fitted to load shotshells.

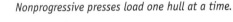

Nonprogressive presses load one hull at a time.

A good progressive press like my RCBS Grand can last a life-time, and that's what I'm expecting. There are enthusiastic folks who will sit down and amortize the price of reloading equipment at three cents per round and tell you how long it will take to pay for that equipment. But in reality, serious handloaders don't actually save money. They simply reinvest their savings into shooting twice as often. And there's definitely something to be said for that.

WHO SHOULD RELOAD?

Reloading is not for everyone, of course. If you must smoke, have distractions nearby, are naturally careless or daring, or if you're the type who doesn't read directions until after you get into trouble, you are much better off purchasing your ammo at Wal-Mart.

A mature, sensible approach is essential. If you understand and have no problem with the fact that components are not interchange-able and that the reloading process must be conducted with extreme care, thought, and precision, you are a candidate for reloading.

THE RELOADING PROCESS

The actual process of loading shotshells is pretty straightforward. What follows is the step-by-step process on a non-progressive press (the simplest available). This type of press can be bought for less than $50, while a high-end progressive press runs $400 to $600. The non-progressive press loads one shell at a time; the shell manually moves from die station to die station until all the operations have been performed. (The owner's manual invariably does a good job of explaining the process, usually with photographs.)

The case body and metal head is full-length resized; the fired primer removed (decapping); a new primer seated (priming); the powder charge dropped; the wad seated; the shot charge dropped; the crimp started; and the final crimp applied. While there may be operational differences among presses, they are likely minor and will be covered in the instructional manual that comes with each press.

The RCBS Grand is a state-of-the-art progressive reloading press.

Progressive presses perform all of the same functions, in the same relative order, as those just outlined, but the functions are performed on each pull of the lever at different stations on different hulls.

The loading process in a progressive press starts with the tool shell plate empty. You insert a case, perform the first step, advance the shell plate, insert a second case, perform two operations, and so on, until the press has six cases in the shell plate—one positioned at each station. After that, you will need to simply keep feeding cases and components in order to obtain a fully loaded round for each down-up stroke of the press handle. The loading process begins at the left front of the tool, progresses counterclockwise, and the finished round is removed from the 9 o'clock position.

Even modest efforts on most non-progressive presses will yield the reloader 100 or more rounds per hour, and some progressives can easily raise the production rate past 250 per hour.

To learn more about the reloading process and to find general suppliers, see the Appendix.

APPENDIX

SHOTGUNS

Benelli-Stoeger-Franchi
17603 Indian Head Highway
Accokeek, MD 20607
301-283-6981
www.benelliusa.com
www.franchiusa.com

Beretta USA
17601 Beretta Drive
Accokeek, MD 20607
301-283-2191
www.berettausa.com

Thomas Bland & Sons
Woodcock Hill, Inc.
192 Spencers Road
P.O. Box 363
Benton, PA 17814
570-864-3242
www.woodcockhill.com

Browning
One Browning Place
Morgan, UT 84050
801-876-2711
www.browning.com

Charles Daly
K.B.I., Inc.
P.O. Box 6625
Harrisburg, PA 17112
866-DALYGUN
www.charlesdaly.com

Connecticut Shotgun Company
35 Woodland Street
New Britain, CT 06501
860-225-6681
www.connecticutshotgun.com

Dakota Arms
1310 Industry Road
Sturgis, SD 57785
605-347-4686
www.dakotaarms.com

European American Armory
P.O. Box 1299
Sharpes, FL 32959
321-639-4842
www.eaacorp.com

Griffin & Howe
36 West 44th Street
Suite 1011
New York, NY 10036
212-921-0980
www.griffinhowe.com

Heckler & Koch, Inc.
(Fabarms)
21480 Pacific Blvd.
Sterling, VA 22170-8903
703-450-1900
www.hecklerkoch-usa.com

Holland & Holland
50 East 57th Street
New York, NY 10022
212-752-7755
www.hollandholland.com

Ithaca Classic Doubles
The Old Station
Number 5 Railroad Street
Victor, NY 14564
585-924-2710
www.ithacadoubles.com

Ithaca Gun
901 Route 34B
King Ferry, NY 13081
888–9-ITHACA
www.ithacagun.com

Krieghoff International
P.O. Box 549
Ottsville, PA 18942
610-847-5173
www.krieghoff.com

Ljutic Industries
732 N. 16th Avenue
Yakima, WA 98902
509-248-0476

Marlin Firearms Co.
100 Kenna Drive
North Haven, CT 06473
203-239-5621
www.marlinfirearms.com

Merkel
GSI, Inc.
7661 Commerce Lane
Trussville, AL 35173
205-655-8299
www.gsifirearms.com

New England Firearms Co., Inc.
(also H&R 1871)
Industrial Rowe
Gardner, MA 01440
978-632-9393

O.F. Mossberg & Sons, Inc.
7 Grasso Avenue
North Haven, CT 06473
203-230-5300
www.mossberg.com

Parker Reproduction Shotguns
114 Broad Street
Flemington, NJ 08822
908-284-2800

Perazzi USA, Inc.
855 North Todd Avenue
Azusa, CA 91741
626-334-1234
perazziusa@aol.com

James Purdey & Sons
57–58 South Audley Street
London
W1K 2ED United Kingdom
Enquries@james-purdey.co.uk

Remington Arms Co., Inc.
870 Remington Drive
P.O. Box 700
Madison, NC 27025-0700
800-243-9700
www.remington.com

Renato Gamba (Carrera)
Rhino
21027 NE Hwy 27
Williston, FL 32696
800-226-3613
rhinoman@atlantic.net

Rizinni SRI
Via 2 Giugno
7/7bis Marcheno
Brescia, Italy 25060
www.rizzini.com

Savage Arms, Inc.
118 Mountain Road
Suffield, CT 06078
800-235-1821
www.savagearms.com

SKB Shotguns
4325 South 120th Street
Omaha, NE 68137
800-752-2767
www.skbshotguns.com

Sturm, Ruger & Co.
200 Ruger Road
Prescott, AZ 86301
520-541-8820
www.ruger-firearms.com

Tar-Hunt Slug Guns
101 Dogtown Road
Bloomsburg, PA 17815
570-784-6368
www.tar-hunt.com

Traditions Performance Firearms
1375 Boston Post Road
Old Saybrook, CT 06475
860-388-4656
www.traditionsfirearms.com

U.S. Repeating Arms
(Winchester Firearms)
275 Winchester Avenue
Morgan, UT 84050-9333
801-876-3440
www.winchester-guns.com

Weatherby, Inc.
3100 El Camino Real
Atascadero, CA 93422
800-227-2016
www.weatherby.com

AMMUNITION

Aguila
Industrias Tecnos S.A.
De C.V. Km
6 Carretera A Tepoztlan
Cuernavaca, Mor. Mexico
52-777-382-14-02
ventas.exp@itecnos.com

All-Purpose Ammo
515 Concord Ind. Drive
Seneca, SC 29672
800-870-2666

Brenneke of America
P.O. Box 1481
Clinton, IA 52733
800-753-9733
www.brennekeusa.com

Bismuth Cartridge Co.
11650 Riverside Drive
N. Hollywood, CA 91602
800-759-3333
www.bismuth-notox.com

Dynamit-Nobel/RWS
81 Ruckman Road
Closter, NJ 07624
201-767-1995
www.dnrws.com

Estate Cartridge
12161 FM 830
Willis, TX 77318
936-856-7277

Federal Cartridge Company
900 Ehlen Drive
Anoka, MN 55303
763-323-3834
www.federalcartridge.com

Fiocchi of America
6930 Fremont Road
Ozark, MO 65721
417-725-4118
www.fiocchiusa.com

Hevi-Shot
EnvironMetal, Inc.
1307 Clark Mill Road
Sweet Home, OR 97386
541-367-3522
Hevishot@aol.com

Hornady Manufacturing
3625 Old Potash Highway
Grand Island, NE 68803
308-382-1390
www.hornady.com

Kent Cartridge
10000 Zigor Road
Kearneysville, WV 25430
888–311-KENT
www.kentgamebore.com

Lightfield Ammunition
P.O. Box 162
Adelphia, NJ 07710
732-462-9200
www.lightfield-ammo.com

Nitro Company Ammunition
7560 Newkirk Road
Mountain Grove, MO 65711
417-746-4600
www.nitrocompany.com

Orion Cartridge Company
Box 1258
Camden, SC 29020
800-642-4110
orion@camden.net

PMC Ammunition
P.O. Box 62508
Boulder City, NV 89006
702-294-0025
www.pmcammo.com

Polywad Shotgun Shells
P.O. Box 7916
Macon, GA 31209
800-998-0669
www.polywad.com

Remington, Inc.
870 Remington Drive
P.O. Box 700
Madison, NC 27025-0700
800-243-9700
www.remington.com

Rio Ammunition
2650 Fountainview, Suite 207
Houston, TX 77057
713-266-3092
www.rioammo.com

Royal Sporting Ltd.
1633 Mount Vernon Road
Dunwoody, GA 30338
800-404-1000
www.royalsportingltd.com

RST Ltd.
7 Weston Way
Center Conway, NH 03813
603-447-6769

Sellier & Bellot, USA
P.O. Box 7307
Shawnee Mission, KS 66207
800-960-2422
ceg@sb-usa.com

Winchester/Olin
427 N. Shamrock Street
East Alton, IL 62024-1174
618-258-2204
www.winchester.com

Wolf Performance Ammunition
2201 E. Winston Road, Suite K
Anaheim, CA 92806
888-757-WOLF
www.wolfammo.com

CHOKE TUBES AND TUBE SETS

Anderson Custom
170 Antioch Road
Batesville, AR 72501
866-307-0500
keith@customshotguns.com

Stan Baker Barrels
10000 Lake City Way
Seattle, WA 98125
206-522-4575

Angle Porting
By Ballistic Specialties
P.O. Box 2401
Batesville, AR 72503
800-276-2550
www.angleport.com

Bansner's Custom Gunsmithing
261 East Main Street
Adamstown, PA 19501
717-484-2370

Briley Manufacturing
1230 Lumpkin
Houston, TX 77043
800-331-5718
www.briley.com

Carlson's
P.O. Box 162
Atwood, KS 67730
785-626-3700

Cation
(Sniper choke tubes)
2341 Alger Street
Troy, MI 48083
810-689-0658
cation@mich.com

Clear View Products
3021 N. Portland
Oklahoma City, OK 73107
405-943-9222

Colonial Arms
1109C Singleton Drive
Selma, AL 36702
800-949-8088
www.colonialarms.com

Comp-N-Choke
925 Waynesboro Highway
Sylvania, GA 30467
888-875-7906
www.comp-n-choke.com

Hastings Barrels
320 Court Street
P.O. Box 224
Clay Center, KS 67432
785-632-2184
www.hastingsbarrels.com

Haydel's Game Calls
5018 Hazel Jones Road
Bossier City, LA 71111
800-HAYDELS
www.haydels.com

Highlander Sports
3004 11th Avenue SW
Huntsville, AL 35805
800-758-2346
curtis@highlandersports.com

Kick's Industries
925 Waynesboro Highway
Sylvania, GA 30467
888-587-2779
www.kicks-ind.com

Lohman Marsh Max
Outland Sports
4500 Doniphan Drive
Neosho, MO 64850
800-922-9034

Marble Arms/Poly-Choke
P.O. Box 111
Gladstone, MI 49837
906-428-3710

Nu-Line Guns
1053 Caulks Hill Road
Harvester, MO 63304
636-441-4500
nulineguns@nulineguns.com

Patternmaster
6431 North Taos Road
Scott City, KS 67871
620-872-3022

Pure Gold Premium
2211 Ogden Road
Rock Hill, SC 29730
803-328-6829
gameacc@cetlimk.net

Rhino Chokes
21890 NE Highway 27
Williston, FL 32696
800-226-3613
rhinoman@atlantic.net

Seminole Gunworks
3049 US Route 1
Mims, FL 32754
800-980-3344
www.seminolegun.com

Truglo
13745 Neutron Drive
Dallas, TX 75244
972-774-0300
www.truglosights.com

Trulock Chokes
102 E. Broad Street
Whigham, GA 31797
800-293-9402
www.trulockchokes.com

Wright's, Inc.
4591 Shotgun Alley
Pinckneyville, IL 62274
618-357-8933
www.wrightschokes.com

SHOOTING ORGANIZATIONS

National Reloading
    Manufacturers Association
One Centerpoint Drive 300
Lake Oswego, OR 97035
www.reload-NRMA.com

National Rifle Association
11250 Waples Mill Road
Fairfax, VA 22030
703-267-1000
www.nra.org

National Shooting Sports
    Foundation
11 Mile Hill Road
Flintlock Ridge Office Center
Newton, CT 06470
203-426-1320
www.nssf.com

National Skeet Shooting
    Association
5931 Roft Road
San Antonio, TX 78253
210-688-3371

National Sporting Clays
    Association
5931 Roft Road
San Antonio, TX 78253
210-688-3371

North American Side-by-Side
    Association
137 Shrewsbury Street
West Boylston, MA 01583
508-835-6057
ewfosterjr.@aol.com

PRO/AM Shotgun Society
P.O. Box 3
Mims, FL 32754
904-345-0485
pass@sportingclays.com

Scholastic Clay Target
    Program
P.O. Box 872
Blacksburg, VA 24063
540-951-1569
wrchristy@mindspring.com

Sporting Arms & Ammunition
    Manufacturers Institute
11 Mile Hill Road
Flintlock Ridge Office Center
Newton, CT 06470
203-426-1320
www.nssf.com

Sporting Clays of America
9257 Buckeye Road
Sugar Grove, OH 43155
740-746-8334

World Sporting Clays Network
2625 Piedmont Road NE
Atlanta, GA 30324
404-266-0202
wcsn@aol.com

GUN-CARE PRODUCTS

Beretta Gallery
718 Madison Avenue
New York, NY 10021
212-319-3235
www.berettausa.com

Birchwood Casey
7900 Fuller Road
Eden Prairie, MN 55344
800-328-6156
www.birchwoodcasey.com

Bore Tech, Inc.
2950 N. Advance Lane
Colmar, PA 18915
215-997-9689
www.boretech.com

BoreSnake
(GunMate)
P.O. Box 1720
Oregon City, OR 97045
503-655-2837

Break-Free, Inc.
An Armor Holdings
13386 International Parkway
Jacksonville, FL 32218
800-428-0588
www.break-free.com

Chem-Pak, Inc.
242 Corning Way
Martinsburg, WV 25401
800-336-9828
www.chem-pak.com

Choke Shine
G.E.M.S., Inc.
33717 Highway 23
Collins, GA 30421
888-507-8762
www.chokeshine.com

Corrosion Technologies
P.O. Box 551625
Dallas, TX 75355-1625
800-638-7361
corrosnx@ix.netcom.com

J. Dewey Rods
P.O. Box 2104
Southbury, CT 06488
203-264-3064

DSX Products
M.S.R., Inc.
P.O. Box 1372
Sterling, VA 20167-1372
800-822-0258

Du-Lite Corporation
171 River Road
Middletown, CT 06457
860-347-2505

EEZOX, Inc.
P.O. Box 772
Waterford, CT 06385
800-462-3331

Flitz International
821 Mohr Avenue
Waterford, WI 53185
800-558-8611
www.flitz.com

Free Gun Cleaner
Frigon Guns
1605 Broughton Road
Clay Center, KS 67432
785-632-5607

Golden Bore Gun Care
Termark International
200 W. 17th Street
Cheyenne, WY 82001
888-483-7677
goldenbore@usa.net

H&R Outdoors
914 Arctic Street
Bridgeport, CT 06608
888-761-4250

Hoppes
Div. of Michaels of Oregon
Airport Industrial Mall
Coatesville, PA 19320
610-384-6000
www.hoppes.com

The Inhibitor
Van Patten Industries
P.O. Box 6694
Rockford, IL 61125
815-332-4812
www.theinhibitor.com

International Lubrication Labs
1895 East 56 Road
Lecompton, KS 66050
785-887-6004

Iosso Products
1485 Lively Boulevard
Elk Grove, IL 60007
847-437-8400
www.iosso.com

Kleen-Bore, Inc.
16 Industrial Parkway
Easthampton, MA 01027
800-445-0301

Mpro7 Gun Care
Windfall, Inc.
P.O. Box 54988

225 W. Deer Valley Road #4
Phoenix, AZ 85078
800-YES-4MP7

Ms Moly Ballistic Conditioner
1952 Knob Road
Burlington, WI 53105
800-264-4140

MTM Molded Products
3370 Obco Court
Dayton, OH 45413
513-890-7461

Neco
536 C. Stone Road
Benicia, CA 94510
707-747-0897

Otis Technology
P.O. Box 582
Lyons Falls, NY 13368
800-OTISGUN
www.otisgun.com

Outers
P.O. Box 38
Onalaska, WI 54650
608-781-5800

Ox-Yoke Originals
34 West Main Street
Milo, ME 04463
207-943-7351

Peak Enterprises
79 Bailey Drive
Newman, GA 30263
770-253-1397
tpeak@west.ga.net

Pro-Shot Products
P.O. Box 763
Taylorsville, IL 62568
217-824-9133
www.proshotproducts.com

Prolix
(Div. Pro-ChemCo)
P.O. Box 1348
Victorville, CA 92393-1348
760-243-3129
prolix@accex.net

ProTec International
1747 Bartlett Road
Memphis, TN 38134
800-843-5649, Ext. 101
sales@proteclubricants.com

Rapid Rod
ATSKO, Inc.
2664 Russell Street
Orangeburg, SC 29115
800-845-2728
info@atsko.com

Rig Products
56 Coney Island Drive
Sparks, NV 89509
775-359-4451

Rusteprufe Labs
1319 Jefferson Avenue
Sparta, WI 54656
608-269-4144
rusteprufe@centurytel.net

Salvo Industries
5173 N. Douglas Fir Road
Calabasas, CA 91302
818-222-2276
jacob@ammotech.com

Sentry Solutions
111 Sugar Hill Road
Contoocook, NH 03229
603-746-5687
bwc@sentrysolutions.com

Shooters Choice Gun Care
Ventco Industries
15050 Berkshire Industrial Parkway
Middlefield, OH 44062
440-834-8888
shooters@shooter-choice.com

Sinclair International
2330 Wayne Haven Street
Fort Wayne, IN 46803
260-493-1858
www.sinclairintl.com

Slip 2000
Superior Products
355 Mandela Parkway
Oakland, CA 94607
707-585-8329
www.slip2000.com

Sports Care Products
P.O. Box 589
Aurora, OH 44202
888-428-8840

TDP Industries
606 Airport Road
Doylestown, PA 18901
215-345-8687

Tetra Gun Care
(FTI, Inc.)
8 Vreeland Road
Florham Park, NJ 07932
973-443-0004

Thunder Products
P.O. Box H
San Jose, CA 95151
408-270-4200

Tipton
Battenfeld Technologies
5885 W. VanHorn Tavern Road
Columbia, MO 65203
877-509-9160
www.battenfeldtechnologies.com

White Lightning
(Leisure Innovations)
1545 Fifth Industrial Court
Bay Shore, NY 11706
800-390-9222

RELOADING EQUIPMENT

Battenfeld Technologies
5875 West Van Horn
    Tavern Road
Columbia, MO 65203
877-509-9160
www.battenfeldtechnologies.com

Brownells, Inc.
200 South Front Street
Montezuma, IA 50171
641-623-5401
www.brownells.com

Dillon Precision
8009 E. Dillon's Way
Scottsdale, AZ 85260
602-948-8009
www.dillonprecision.com

Hornady Manufacturing
Box 1848
Grand Island, NE 68802
308-382-1390

Lee Precision
4275 Highway U
Hartford, WI 53027
262-673-3075

MEC
Mayfield Engineering
715 South Street
Mayville, WI 53050
920-387-4500
www.mecreloaders.com

Midway USA
5875 West Van Horn
  Tavern Road
Columbia, MO 65203
573-445-6363
www.midwayusa.com

Ponsness/Warren
768 Ohio Street
Rathdrum, ID 83858
208-687-2231
bsteele@reloaders.com

RCBS
P.O. Box 39
Onalaska, WI 54650
800-635-7656
www.outers-guncare.com

Spolar Power Load
2273 S. Vista B-2
Bloomington, CA 92316
800-227-9667
www.spolargold.com

POWDERS AND RELOADING COMPONENTS

Accurate Arms
5891 Highway 230 West
McEwen, TN 37101
800-416-3006
www.accuratepowder.com

ADCO/NobelSport
4 Draper Street
Woburn, MA 01801
781-935-1799
www.adcosales.com

Alaskan Cartridge
RR2 Box 192F
Hastings, NE 68901-9408
402-463-3415

Alliant Powder Company
P.O. Box 4
State Rte. 114
Radford, VA 21141-0096
800-276-9337
dick-quesenberry@atk.com

Ball Powder Propellant
(Street Marks Powder)
P.O. Box 222
Street Marks, FL 32355
850-577-2273
srfaintich@stm.gd-ots.com

Ballistic Products, Inc.
P.O. Box 293
Hamel, MN 55340
763-494-9237
www.ballisticproducts.com

Claybuster Wads
C&D Special Products
309 Sequoya Drive
Hopkinsville, KY 42240
502-885-8088
dmac@spis.net

Clean Shot Technologies
21218 Street Andrews Blvd #504
Boca Raton, FL 33433
888-419-2073
cleanshot@aol.com

Duster Wads
Micro Technologies
1405 Laukant Street
Reedsburg, WI 53959
888-438-7837

Hodgdon Powder
6231 Robinson
Shawnee Mission, KS 66201
913-362-9455
info@hodgdon.com

IMR Powder
6733 Mississauga Road
Suite 306
Mississauga, Ontario
Canada L5N 6J5
520-393-1600
www.imrpowder.com

Lawrence Brand Shot
Metalico-Granite City
1200 16th Street
Granite City, IL 62040
618-451-4400

Polywad Spred-R
P.O. Box 7916
Macon, GA 31209
800-998-0669
www.polywad.com

Reloading Specialties
52901 265th Avenue
Pine Island, MN 55963
507-356-8500

Vihtavuori/Lapua
Kalton-Pettibone
1241 Ellis Street
Bensenville, IL 60106
800-683-0464
jbolda@kaltron.com

RamShot Powders
Western Powders
P.O. Box 158
Yellowstone Hill
Miles City, MT 59301
800-497-1007
powder@midrivers.com

SHOOTING SCHOOLS

AAClaybusters, LLC
Seattle, WA
877-783-4576
aaclaybusters@att.net

Addieville East Farm
Maplesville, RI 02839
401-568-3185
www.addieville.com

Arnold's Custom Shooting
Sports
Camden, OH 45311
937-787-3352
www.customshooting.com

LL Bean Shooting School
Freeport, ME 04032
888-552-3261

Bender Shima Shooting
Clinics
Alpharetta, GA 30005
678-296-5184
bender285@aol.com

Big Moore's Run Lodge
Coudersport, PA 16915
866-569-3474

Blackwater Training Company
Moyock, NC 27958
252-435-2488
billm@blackwaterlodge.com

Pete Blakeley Shooting School
Lewisville, TX 75057
972-462-0043
www.dallasgunclub.com

British School of Shooting
Saint Simons Island, GA 31522
912-656-1587
jonestheshoot@aol.com

Broxton Bridge Plantation
Ehrhardt, SC 29081
800-437-4868

Deep River Shooting School
Sanford, NC 27330
919-774-7080
www.deepriver.net

Elite Shooting School
Houston, TX 77063
713-334-0656
elitegun@aol.com

Buz Fawcett's Wingshooting
Meridian, ID 83642
208-888-3415

FieldSport
Traverse City, MI 49684
231-933-0767
www.fieldsportltd.com

Connie Fournier/ISA
Bethel Park, PA
412-835-5749
gunteach@bellatlantic.net

Friar Tuck Wing & Clay School
Catskill, NY 12414
800-832-7600, Ext. 447
www.friartuckswingandclay.com

Les Greevy's West Branch
    Shooting School
Williamsport, PA 17701
570-326-6561
greevy@mail.microserve.net

Griffin & Howe Shooting
    Schools
Bernardsville, NJ 07924
908-766-2287
www.griffinhowe.com

Jo Hanley Shooting Instruction
West Palm Beach, FL 33407
561-881-8323
joshot@excelonline.com

Holland & Holland Sporting
New York, NY 10022
212-752-7755
www.hollandandholland.com

The Homestead Shooting School
Hot Springs, VA 24445
540-839-7787

Hunter's Creek Club
Metamora, MI 48455
810-664-4307
www.hunterscreekclub.com

Instinctive Target Interception
Shotgun Shooting School
Albuquerque, NM 87120
505-836-1206
itishooting@juno.com

Instructional Shooting
Lowell, MA 01852
978-452-8450
www.agguns.com

J&P Shooting School
Sudlersville, MD 21668
410-438-3832
staff@jphuntinglodge.com

Jamison Shotgun Sports
Denver, CO 80231
303-745-3840

Joshua Creek Ranch
Boerne, TX 78881
830-537-5090
www.joshuacreek.com

Phil Kiner Trapshooting Clinics
Cheyenne, WY 82001
307-635-1451

John Kruger Shooting
   Enterprises
Sunman, IN 47001
812-926-4999
www.quailridgeclub.com

Longshot Shooting School
Broken Arrow, OK 74014
800-348-1111

Keith Lupton Shooting Schools
Dover Plains, NY 12522
845-877-3719

Middleditch Shooting School
Orlando, FL 32822
407-380-9533

Midwest Shooting School
Wrenshall, MN 55797
218-384-3670
www.midwestshootingschool.com

Dan Mitchell's Clay and Wingshooting School
Gervais, OR 97026
503-792-3431
danidaho@insn.com

Michael Murphy & Sons
Augusta, KS 67010
316-775-2137
www.murphyshotguns.com

National Wing & Clay School
Woodland, WA 98674
360-225-5000
info@shootinginstruction.com

Kay Ohye Trap School
North Brunswick, NJ 08902
732-297-0364

On Target
Yorba Linda, CA 92886
714-970-8072
jbraccini@aol.com

Optimum Shotgun Performance
   Shooting School
Houston, TX 77070
281-897-0800
www.ospschool.com

Orvis Shooting Schools
Manchester, VT 05254
800-235-9763
www.orvis.com

Outdoors Unlimited Shooting
School
Eagle Lake, TX 77434
979-234-5750

Paragon School of Sporting
Flat Rock, NC 28731
828-693-6600
www.paragonschool.com

Peace Dale Shooting School
Peace Dale, RI 02871
401-789-3730
pdshootrichf@aol.com

Gary Phillips Shooting
Instruction
Wilmington, DE 19806
302-655-7113
gphilgun1@aol.com

Pintail Point Shooting School
Queenstown, MD 21658
410-827-7029
www.pintailpoint.com

Prairie Moon Ranch
San Antonio, TX 78009
210-732-8765
www.clayschool.com

Remington Shooting School
WRA Services
Excelsior, MN 55331
800-742-7053
www.remingtonshoot-
ingschool.com

Rock Run Sports Club
Coatesville, PA 19320
610-383-1000
www.rockrunclub.com

Safari Club Wingshooting
School
Rochester, NY 14620
Steve Schultz
585-473-4111
wwwsafariclub.org

Sea Island Shooting School
Sea Island, GA 31561
1-800-Sea-Island
1-800-732-4752
bobedwards@seaisland.com

Shoot Where You Look
Livingston, TX 77351
800-201-5535

Shooting Academy at
Nemacolin Woodlands
Resort and Spa
Farmington, PA 15437
800-422-2736
www.nemacolin.com

TM Ranch Shotgun Sports
Orlando, FL 32822
407-737-3788
tmranch@bellsouth.net

Taddlinger's Shooting School
Wilmington, VT 05363
802-464-1223

Texas Academy
Texas Wingshooting Sports
Whitewright, TX 75491
903-364-2076
texaspa2@gte.net

Thunder Ranch
Mountain Home, TX 78058
830-640-3138

Angelo Troisi Skeet Shooting
  Clinic
Andover, MA 01810
978-470-3481
shinespapa@mediaone.net

The Willow
Robinsville, MS 38664
662-357-3154
danielsb@grandcasinos.com

Wise Wingshooting Academy
Chestertown, MD 21620
410-778-4950
benwise@friend.ly.net

Woodcock Hill
Benton, PA 17814
570-864-3242
bland@epix.net

OTHER CONTACTS

American Gunsmithing Institute
1325 Imola Avenue, W. 504
Napa, CA 94559
707-253-0462
www.americangunsmith.com

Black's Wing & Clay Directory
P.O. Box 2029
Red Bank, NJ 07701
732-224-8700
blacksporting@msn.com

Second Skin Camo
3434 Buck Mt. Road
Roanoke, VA 24014
540-774-9248
www.trebark.com

INDEX